Through the Bible In 12 Weeks

The Big Picture Experience

By Jenny Baker

Group

Group resources actually work!

This Group resource incorporates our R.E.A.L. approach to ministry. It reinforces a growing friendship with Jesus, encourages long-term learning, and results in life transformation, because it's

Relational
Learner-to-learner interaction enhances learning and builds Christian friendships.

Experiential
What learners experience through discussion and action sticks with them up to 9 times longer than what they simply hear or read.

Applicable
The aim of Christian education is to equip learners to be both hearers and doers of God's Word.

Learner-based
Learners understand and retain more when the learning process takes into consideration how they learn best.

Through the Bible
12 Lessons to Help Students Navigate the Big Picture

Credits
Senior Editor: Candace McMahan
Acquisitions Editors: Rick Lawrence, Patty Smith
Editor: Kelli B. Trujillo
Chief Creative Officer: Joani Schultz
Copy Editor: Janis Sampson
Art Director: Jeff A. Storm
Cover Designer: Jeff A. Storm
Book Designer/ Print Production Artist: Riley Hall
Production Manager: DeAnne Lear

Unless otherwise indicated, all Scripture quotations are taken from the Holy Bible, New Living Translation, copyright © 1996, 2004, 2007. Used by permission of Tyndale House Publishers, Inc., Carol Stream, Illinois 60188. All rights reserved.

ISBN: 978-0-7644-3891-2

10 9 8 7 6 5 4 3 2 1   18 17 16 15 14 13 12 11 10 09
Printed in the United States of America.

Table of Contents

Introduction: How to Use These Studies

This 12-week study series will give your teenagers an overview of the "big story" of the Bible. They'll develop an understanding that this strange assortment of ancient books is all interlinked, purposeful, intentional, and part of an ongoing adventure! These studies will help them understand God's interactions with people throughout the history of the world, beginning from Creation to the present day and into the future. They'll help young people locate themselves within this big story as they come to understand God's plans and purposes in their lives and respond to God's invitation to be part of his kingdom. Through these experiences with you, your teenagers will gain a deep understanding that they are part of this story and its continuation—that their roots go back to Creation and their future can be in the new creation! And they'll move beyond just learning about the Bible—they'll have opportunities to personally encounter the author of the big story: God.

The Studies

Engage

Ultimately, it starts with you. Before you teach your group about each theme, idea, or passage, you need to take some time to explore it on your own—to have your own personal encounter with the God of the Bible. So at the start of each session, you'll find Engage, a short devotion written just for you to help you engage with the biblical story and reflect on how God is leading and challenging you. I hope that communicating this amazing story will impact you, too—that you'll get caught up in the big picture and have a fresh vision for your place in the ongoing story of God's interactions with humanity. So be sure each week to spend time with God, listening to what he has to say to you from his story.

Life-Changing Learning

What was the last new thing you learned and how did you learn it? There's an old and well-known saying attributed to Confucius, that goes, "I hear and I forget; I see and I remember; I do and I understand." Is that true in your experience?

Often when we're communicating Christian truth, we use lots of words and expect our audience to just listen to them and take them all in. And while there's a time and a place for lectures, sermons, and motivational speeches, youth group meetings are not usually it! When teenagers come to your youth group, it's not for a school-like experience. They want to have fun, be engaged and involved, express their opinions, and discover new things.

So each week during this study series, you'll lead teenagers through experiential learning activities—games, object lessons, discussions with partners, hands-on projects, private meditation, and other activities that will invite the teenagers in your group to explore, think, interact, and feel. Many of the activities and discussion questions are intentionally open-ended. Not everyone will draw the same conclusions—and that's OK! Don't feel like you have to explain absolutely everything or get your teenagers to rationalize what they have experienced. Sometimes we all need time to mull over our experiences, to live with the mystery and the questions until we reach our own conclusions—that *eureka* moment when we see things far more clearly for ourselves! So leave things open-ended and allow room for God to work…your teenagers may even surprise you with their observations and insights.

Group Size

You can use these studies at home with a small group of six teenagers, in the church gym with 100 teenagers, or anything in between! The activities are created to be flexible for different group sizes. And when special modifications are needed, look for a Tip box in the margin that will give you specific ideas for how to change the experience to fit the size of your group.

Experiencing the Story

Every study begins with an opportunity for teenagers to do something unique and fun called Experience the Story. Though these parts of the study don't overtly connect to Scripture and don't involve Bible teaching, they do set the stage for what the teenagers in your group are about to learn. These experiences are what will draw your teenagers in and get them ready to think, chew on, and engage with God's Word in a truly meaningful way.

Telling the Story

Each study includes a Tell the Story element in which you'll connect the biblical narrative to the activities the group has just done. These sections involve discussion as well as some teaching from you. Take time to learn what you need to communicate; in the studies you'll find descriptions of the key points you need to cover as well as samples of how you may want to say things. But don't use our suggestions as a script! Digest the main ideas we've included, and then teach using your own words.

In each of these sessions, one or more teenagers will read Scripture aloud, and this icon will clue you in. Do your best to have plenty of Bibles on hand so that every teenager is able to flip through a Bible and read along. The goal here is to get teenagers comfortable with looking into Scripture on their own—rather than just listening to others read it. If you've got a fair amount of young people who are not familiar with the Bible, be ready to point out page numbers of specific passages, or mark passages ahead of time with sticky notes.

Connecting the Story

In studies 2-11, you'll include a short Connect the Story element that helps teenagers visualize the main point of the story for that day. You'll do this by using a large white poster board each week to create a "page" that's part of the "big story." This section not only covers the theme, but it also gives you a chance to introduce your group to all the books of the Bible and to familiarize them with each biblical genre. You'll keep each poster that's created and will use it in the final session (12) to help your group recap the whole scope of the big story together.

Respond to the Story

Every session also includes projects, discussions, and other experiences that allow for teenagers to Respond to the Story by reflecting on the theme of the study and considering how it applies directly to their own lives.

You'll equip teenagers to take this even further by giving them a weekly Take-Home Devotion (see pages 154-159). These take-home devos will help teenagers spend some time on their own during the week, looking more deeply into the topic and taking a step that puts their ideas into action. As part of these devotions, teenagers will be encouraged to write their thoughts in journals and do some other simple activities. If you can, purchase spiral notebooks, and pass them out at the end of

Study 1; or encourage your group members to use their own notebooks or blank books as journals during the series. Every week, as you pass out the devotion, prompt each teenager to take the page home and tape or glue it into a journal.

Meditate and Memorize

Every study outline begins and ends with a Key Passage of Scripture that encapsulates the study's core message. You can use the Key Passage as a memory verse for your group or incorporate it into your study time in other creative ways; you'll find ideas at the end of each study session for ways you can tie in the Key Passage.

Supplies

Near the start of each study, you'll find a list of the specific supplies you need to use and what copies you need to make from the photocopiable sheets in the Appendix (pp. 153-187); but just so you can plan ahead, here's a big-picture look at what you'll need:

General Supplies for Use in Each Study

- ❑ Bibles
- ❑ paper and pens or pencils
- ❑ iPod or CD player for background music

Study 1

- ❑ 5 to 10 pads of sticky notes (or more)
- ❑ 1 large piece of white poster board
- ❑ several rolls of tape
- ❑ paper bag or bowl
- ❑ photocopies of "How Does It End?" (p. 160), "Characters" (p. 163), and "Story" (p. 154), prepared according to study instructions

Study 2

- ❑ small garbage can
- ❑ modeling dough or clay (alternate supplies: several sheets of paper, crayons)
- ❑ 1 or more plastic trays or place mats
- ❑ plastic building blocks and some model instructions (alternate supplies: square-cut paper, origami instructions)
- ❑ optional: TV, DVD player, nature DVD (such as the Discovery Channel/BBC series "Planet Earth" or a National Geographic video)
- ❑ optional: butcher paper or white poster board, colored markers
- ❑ optional: cushions
- ❑ 1 large piece of white poster board
- ❑ 1 envelope
- ❑ photocopies of "Relationship Cross" (p. 169), "Who Made…" quiz (pp. 166-167), "Who Made…" quiz answers (p. 168), and "Source" (p. 154), prepared according to study instructions

Study 3

- ❑ several sets of earplugs
- ❑ several blindfolds
- ❑ card-stock Relationship Cross used in Study 2 (also on p. 169)
- ❑ 1 large piece of white poster board
- ❑ 1 black marker
- ❑ variety of paper and art supplies, such as pieces of card stock, acrylic or tempera paint, watercolor paint, paintbrushes, magazines, scissors, glue, colored pencils, crayons, construction paper, scraps of fabric, magazines, craft sticks
- ❑ newspaper or plastic tarp
- ❑ photocopies of "Top Critics" (p. 170) and "Broken" (p. 155), prepared according to study instructions

Study 4

- ❑ adult volunteer
- ❑ several large pop-culture posters (movie and band, for example)
- ❑ large paper or plastic bag
- ❑ several rolls of various kinds of tape (duct, transparent, masking)
- ❑ delicious cake or brownies (homemade if possible)
- ❑ plates, napkins, and silverware (or plastic ware)
- ❑ dirtied bowl and cooking supplies
- ❑ dish soap, sponges, dish towels
- ❑ sink for washing dishes
- ❑ 1 large piece of white poster board
- ❑ 3 large sheets of newsprint or flip-chart paper
- ❑ red, yellow, and green sticky dots
- ❑ tape (to affix the newsprint sheets to the wall)
- ❑ photocopies of "The Ten Commandments" (p. 171) and "Invitation" (p. 155), prepared according to study instructions

Study 5

- [ ] clock
- [ ] exercise supplies and silly challenge supplies (as needed); see study instructions.
- [ ] tempting items, like ice-cold soda, candy bars, other treats, cell phone, pillow, comfy chair, on so on
- [ ] paper bag or bowl
- [ ] large sheets of newsprint or butcher paper
- [ ] tape
- [ ] colored markers (not black)
- [ ] 1 big black marker
- [ ] 1 large piece of white poster board
- [ ] photocopies of "The Kings (and Queens) of the Bible" (p. 172), "Idols Today" (p. 174), and "Choice" (p. 156), prepared according to study instructions

Study 6

- [ ] 5 different colored pieces of poster board or card stock
- [ ] tape
- [ ] 1 large piece of white poster board
- [ ] glue
- [ ] photocopies of "Shades of Emotions" (p. 175), "I Need Advice" (p. 176), "Write Your Own Psalm" (p. 178), and "Reality" (p. 156), prepared according to study instructions

Study 7

- [ ] 4 different types of snacks
- [ ] 3 adult volunteers
- [ ] plastic bags, paper plates, and napkins
- [ ] your cell phone and an adult volunteer with another cell phone
- [ ] large sheets of card stock or card board, cut into speech-bubble shapes
- [ ] old magazines, scissors, glue, markers
- [ ] 1 large piece of white poster board
- [ ] photocopies of "Communication" (p. 157), prepared according to study instructions

Study 8

- [ ] markers, tape, scissors
- [ ] makeup, hair straightener and/or curling iron, hairspray, dress-up clothes, accessories
- [ ] old magazines, scissors, glue, a large sheet of butcher paper or card stock, pens, markers
- [ ] 1 large piece of white poster board
- [ ] sunflower seeds (in shells)
- [ ] bowl
- [ ] white glue
- [ ] marker
- [ ] photocopies of the "Model Station Instructions" (p. 181), "Character Cards" (p. 183), "Model Template" (p. 182), and "Challenge" (p. 157), prepared according to study instructions

Study 9

- [ ] Relationship Cross (p. 169) from Study 3
- [ ] 5 to 15 helium balloons
- [ ] heavy card stock, cut into lengthwise strips
- [ ] several staplers
- [ ] pens
- [ ] scissors
- [ ] 1 large black garbage bag
- [ ] 1 large piece of white poster board
- [ ] photocopies of "Failure?" (p. 185) and "Solution" (p. 158), prepared according to study instructions

Study 10

- [ ] several pads of sticky notes
- [ ] crayons
- [ ] tape
- [ ] random objects from your meeting room or brought from home
- [ ] 7 sheets of newsprint or flip-chart paper
- [ ] 2-foot leather cord for every student
- [ ] 7 beads (that fit on cord) for every student
- [ ] some extra beads and cord
- [ ] 1 large piece of white poster board
- [ ] photocopies of "Prayer Cord" (p. 187) and "Life" (p. 158), prepared according to study instructions

Study 11	Study 12
❑ The Day After Tomorrow DVD or similar film (see suggestions on p. 139) ❑ TV and DVD player ❑ student art pieces saved from Study 3 ❑ newspapers and magazines ❑ materials for junk modeling: cardboard boxes, duct tape, masking tape, aluminum foil, scissors, glue, twine, metal clothes hangers, other random pieces of junk ❑ basic art supplies, like markers, tempera paints, glitter-glue pens, construction paper ❑ 1 large piece of white poster board ❑ photocopies of "Hope" (p. 159), prepared according to study instructions	❑ all 11 "pages" of the story—the poster-board pieces you created during each Connect the Story segment ❑ optional: tape ❑ lots of celebratory food and drinks, like pizza, soda, ice cream ❑ samples of other Bible study materials teenagers could use in the future ❑ optional: new Bibles to give to teenagers as a way to mark their journey through God's Word

Plan Ahead

Be sure to plan ahead for these activities:

- If you can, purchase a blank book or spiral-bound notebook for every teenager in your group to use as a journal during this study series.

- In Study 4, teenagers will try to reassemble torn up posters. Take a shopping trip ahead of time to get totally cheesy teenage (or preteen) posters as well as some cool pop-culture posters. These posters will be destroyed in the study, so buy inexpensive ones.

- In Study 5, you'll need to borrow some exercise equipment. Call a few families from your church ahead of time to see if they can lend fitness equipment to your group.

- In Study 7, you'll need a bunch of pop-culture magazines (news, sports, entertainment magazines, and so on). Contact 5 to 10 adults in church at the start of the series, and ask them to save magazines over the next few weeks that they can donate to the youth group. The more magazines you get, the better.

- In Study 8, some teenagers will give a volunteer a makeover, so have a few teenagers bring their beauty supplies, like curling irons, makeup, and so forth.

- In Study 11, teenagers will create models and sculptures using "junk" (like cardboard boxes). Check with the parents of some of your teenagers early on in the study series, and ask if they can save some junk for your group to use. If a few families save some materials for you over a few weeks, you should get plenty of junk for the activity!

- In Study 12, we recommend that you give a new Bible to each student. Check with your church leaders to see if the funds are available to make this purchase.

1 STORY

Aims

This study will help teenagers

- discover that there is a coherent metanarrative—a big story—running through the Bible.

- understand that God has been involved with people and creation throughout history.

- realize that we are part of the "final act of the play"—the story continues beyond the Bible text to our lives.

Key Passage

"All Scripture is inspired by God and is useful to teach us what is true and to make us realize what is wrong in our lives. It corrects us when we are wrong and teaches us to do what is right. God uses it to prepare and equip his people to do every good work."

- 2 Timothy 3:16-17

Overview

Experience the Story	25 minutes	In teams of four, teenagers are given the start of a story and the characters in it. They then have to create an ending to the story and act it out.
Tell the Story	20 minutes	In pairs and as a large group, teenagers will creatively explore various opinions about the Bible. You'll introduce the idea of the big story of the Bible and explain what this study is about.
Respond to the Story	15 minutes	Group members will get to know some of the main "characters" in the Bible and will consider their own roles in God's big story. They'll write down their questions and opinions about the Bible during a time of reflection.

Supplies

Make sure you've got

- ❑ Bibles
- ❑ photocopies of the "How Does It End?" handout (p. 160), 1 per student
- ❑ 5 to 10 pads of sticky notes (or more)
- ❑ pens or pencils
- ❑ 1 large piece of white poster board with the word "Story" written in large letters in the middle. (Keep this poster for the final study.)
- ❑ tape (to affix "Story" poster to the wall during the study)
- ❑ photocopies of "Characters" handout (p. 163), cut apart. You'll need approximately 1 copy for every 5 teenagers.
- ❑ several rolls of tape
- ❑ paper bag or bowl
- ❑ iPod or CD player for ambient background music
- ❑ photocopies of "Story" take-home handout (p. 154), cut apart, 1 per student

Before the Study

Prepare photocopies of "How Does It End?" (p. 160), "Characters" (p. 163), and "Story" (p. 154). Put all the cut-apart strips from "Characters" in a bag or bowl. Take some time to personally engage with the theme of this study by using the Scripture reflection suggestions below.

Engage

Before the study, set aside some time and space for you to reflect on and engage with the story on a personal level.

Read 2 Timothy 3:14-17. Think about your experience of the Bible—how you were taught about it, how you've read it, what it means to you. Now take a piece of paper and on one side list all the blessings that the Bible has brought to your life and your other positive associations with it. For example, you may think of specific passages that have shaped your life, or people who have taught it to you well, or people who have provided a positive example for you of what it looks like to really read and study Scripture.

Then on the other side of the paper list any negative experiences or associations you've had regarding the Bible. For example, you may think of passages that you've struggled with, Scriptures that have been misinterpreted or taught to you incorrectly, or feelings of guilt you've experienced for not reading it enough.

Now read 2 Timothy 3:14-17 again. Bring both the positive and negative aspects of your experience of the Bible to God in prayer. Be honest with how you feel about the Bible. Ask God to open up his Word to you so that it will equip you for your part in the kingdom of God.

Pray for your group:
Thank God for the power of his Word, and pray that the teenagers you work with will get excited about God's Word.

Experience the Story

(about 25 minutes)

Welcome teenagers as they arrive; then help them form teams of four. Hand out copies of "How Does It End?", one per person. Invite volunteers to read the character descriptions aloud, and explain that in each team of four, teenagers will each select and play one of these characters. Let everybody know that they can change the gender of the characters as needed to fit their group. (If you've got some teams of three, they can drop one of the characters; if there are teams of five, have teenagers make up their own new character and add him or her to the story.) Explain that there are four acts of the play already written; it will be their job to work in their teams to come up with the ending of the story: the fifth act. Stress that as they develop their final act, they need to stay true to the characters as they've been described and how they've behaved in the first four acts of the story. Characters can change and develop in the story, but they need to have a reason to do so.

Prompt teams to find a space to sit together away from the rest of the group. Have team members read aloud the descriptions of the first four acts of the play, and then give teams 10 to 15 minutes to work out and practice their endings to the play.

The four acts of the story that teenagers will explore together broadly follow the structure of the biblical story. In Act 1, the friends create something good they're excited about. There's a parallel here with the world God created. In Act 2, it seems like everything has gone wrong—echoing the Fall. In Act 3, they try to sort things out for themselves, but it just doesn't work. This is a bit like Israel trying to keep the commandments and live in God's ways. Act 4 portrays a teacher offering a way to sort things out—a little like Jesus' intervention in and redemption of the world. The teens themselves have to complete Act 5, rather like the task before us to live faithfully in God's world. Teenagers probably won't recognize the similarity to the biblical narrative and that's OK—these themes will be reinforced throughout the studies over the next several weeks.

After 10 to 15 minutes, invite the teams to present their endings to the rest of the group. After all the presentations, compliment them on their imagination and creativity. Discuss these questions together:

- In your opinion, which endings were most realistic or least realistic? Why?

- How challenging was it to come up with a fitting ending? Explain.

- Did you think it was difficult to stay true to your character? Why or why not?

TIP If you're doing this study with a large number of teenagers, have the small groups pair up to show each other their fifth acts rather than having each team of four present their ending to the entire group.

Tell the Story
(about 20 minutes)

Say something like: *You just acted out the ending of a story. You read the first four acts, got inside the skin of your characters, and made up an ending. But it wasn't just any old ending. Your characters couldn't suddenly become superheroes, or win the lottery on a Thursday, or escape in their private jet to the Caribbean. This had to be real, to suit the people and the place. It had to make sense. It had to fit.*

All of us need to write the ending of our own stories in life. There are lots of different opinions about the best way to live your life; we all have a big story that explains for us what life is about. Some people make earning money their goal. Their story says that being rich is the way to be happy and to live life to the full. Some people want to be famous. Their aim is to be on the front pages of the magazines, to be celebrated for being a celebrity. Others go after power. If they are in charge, then they can write the story of their lives exactly as they want it to be.

Hang up the poster board that says "Story" on the wall right behind you so everyone can see it; then continue teaching, saying something like:

But what if there was another story? What if someone had already written out the beginning of the story, and you just had to find your place in it? What if you could see what life was all about, how it began, how it's developed, why things have gone wrong, and how they can be sorted out? What if we could learn from everyone else's mistakes? What if we could get some advice from the designer of life itself?

The Bible may seem like an ancient and out-of-date book. Some Bibles are just text, have strange columns, weirdly thin paper, and no pictures. What if the Bible—the text of God's big story—can help us understand our own stories?

Have teens form new pairs (with people who weren't in their acting team), and give each pair a pen and at least six sticky notes. Invite pairs to discuss these questions:

- What are the most common opinions out there in our culture about the Bible? What are some of the positive opinions? What are some of the negative opinions?

- What different opinions about the Bible do people have at your school? in your family?

Direct pairs to work together to write at least six different opinions about the Bible on their ten sticky notes, each starting with the words "The Bible is…" Challenge them to write realistic opinions—perhaps things they've actually heard other people say. Also encourage them to try to cover a wide spectrum of opinions, from positive to neutral to negative.

Once pairs have written their six opinions, have them exchange what they've written with another pair.

Designate a wall in your meeting space as an opinion spectrum. Point out that one end of the wall is for negative opinions, the opposite end is for positive opinions, and the middle is for neutral or lukewarm opinions. Instruct pairs to stick each of their opinion sticky notes on the wall wherever they think is most appropriate.

Invite everyone to read the various sticky notes on the wall, and then ask:

- Which opinions stand out to you most? Why?

- Which opinions do you most strongly agree with or disagree with? Why?

Say something like: *Let's look at how the Bible describes itself.*

Invite a student to read aloud 2 Timothy 3:16-17, and then ask the group:

- How do these ideas compare with what's on our opinion wall?

- Do you think most people would agree or disagree with the ideas in 2 Timothy 3:16-17? Explain.

Explain to the group that Christians believe the secret of life is in the Bible. They believe that this ancient book is true and that they should base their lives on it. Tell the group that over the next several weeks, you'll explore together what the Bible is all about and how it relates to us. Let them know that you're not going to tell them what to believe about the Bible or about God, but rather that you want to help them understand what the Bible is all about so they can each make up their own mind about it.

Respond to the Story
(about 15 minutes)

Play some ambient music in the background as you pass around the bag (or bowl) containing strips from the "Characters" handout. Invite everyone to take three or four strips from the bag. Explain that the names on the strips are names of people in the Bible—people they might have heard about and people who may be new to them. Say something like: *These are people in the Bible who are part of God's story. How are they like you? How are they different?*

Invite them to spend some time reading the strips they've received and then, using small pieces of tape, add them to the wall of sticky notes. Prompt teenagers to read some of the character names and descriptions that the others are adding to the wall.

Then ask teenagers to think about how they fit into God's story. Set out several more pads of sticky notes and pens by the wall, and direct teenagers to take sticky notes and write their thoughts about the Bible and God's story. Invite them to consider how they feel at the start of this study series. What are their expectations? Can they see any links between themselves and the characters on the wall? What questions do they have about the Bible? What do they want to say to God about the Bible? Encourage them to approach this freely, writing whatever they'd like in response to what you've discussed so far.

Direct teens to stick their sticky notes on the wall as a way of saying they're up for exploring the big story of the Bible and discovering what it can mean in their own lives.

After adequate time for teenagers to think, read, and write, wrap up the meeting with a short prayer. Pass out the "Story" take-home handouts, one per student. Invite teenagers to set aside about 15 minutes (or more) during the week to explore the story more deeply on their own using the handout. Explain that they each can tape the handout into a notebook that can serve as an exploration journal throughout the series. They can use their exploration journals as their own personal space for writing down their questions and thoughts.

Each week you'll pass out a take-home handout that will guide teenagers in personal reflection and journaling during the week. If you can, purchase some spiral-bound notebooks or blank books that your teenagers can use as their journals during this series.

Key Passage

"All Scripture is inspired by God and is useful to teach us what is true and to make us realize what is wrong in our lives. It corrects us when we are wrong and teaches us to do what is right. God uses it to prepare and equip his people to do every good work."

- 2 Timothy 3:16-17

This Key Passage can help teenagers grasp the main idea of the study. You can use it in different ways, such as

- writing it on a poster and hanging the poster up in your meeting space,

- projecting it on a screen,

- inviting teenagers to write it on blank business cards that they can keep in their wallets or pockets,

- prompting teenagers to write it on sticky notes and stick the notes on their mirrors or nightstands at home, or

- challenging teenagers to memorize it on their own during the week.

2 SOURCE

Aims

This study will help teenagers

- understand that God made a good, functioning world for us to live in.

- appreciate the scope of Creation—not just the natural world, but also everything else that has been developed from it.

- consider their roles as beings uniquely created by God.

Key Passage

"Then God looked over all he had made, and he saw that it was very good! And evening passed and morning came, marking the sixth day. So the creation of the heavens and the earth and everything in them was completed."

- Genesis 1:31–2:1

Overview

Experience the Story, Part 1	10 minutes	Participants will draw their ideal world but every so often pass their pictures to the people on their left who add to them.
Experience the Story, Part 2	20 minutes	Teenagers will spend time at stations, exploring themes of creation.
Tell the Story	15 minutes	The group will learn what the Bible says about God creating a good, functioning world for us to live in.
Connect the Story	10 minutes	Teenagers will collaborate to make a collage of words, symbols, and cartoons summarizing the Creation story.
Respond to the Story	5 minutes	Teenagers will be led through a time of quiet reflection and consider God's role in creating them each as unique individuals.

Supplies

Make sure you've got

- ☐ Bibles
- ☐ paper and pens
- ☐ photocopies of "Who Made…" quiz (p. 166-167), 1 per student
- ☐ 1 copy of "Who Made…" quiz answers (p. 168) in an envelope
- ☐ small trash can
- ☐ several large lumps of modeling dough or clay. (Alternate supplies if you don't have modeling dough or clay: several sheets of paper, crayons.)
- ☐ 1 or more plastic trays or place mats (to place clay models on)
- ☐ plastic building blocks and some model instructions. (Alternate supplies if you don't have plastic building blocks: several sheets of paper cut square; a book about how to fold origami models or printouts of origami instructions from the Internet.)

- ❑ optional: TV, DVD player, nature DVD (such as the Discovery Channel/BBC series "Planet Earth" or a National Geographic video).
- ❑ optional: large sheet of butcher paper or white poster board; colored markers
- ❑ optional: cushions
- ❑ photocopy of "Relationship Cross" (p. 169) on heavy card stock
- ❑ iPod or CD player for instrumental background music
- ❑ 1 large piece of poster board with the word "Source" written in large letters at the top. (Keep this poster for the final study.)
- ❑ photocopies of "Source" take-home handout (p. 154), cut apart, 1 per student

Before the Study

Create three or four stations in your meeting area that teenagers will explore during "Experience the Story, Part 2." A station is simply a place with materials or experiences that help participants focus on an idea. A station can be set up on a tabletop, on the floor, or in a corner. If you want, you can set out some cushions at each one to encourage them to linger and engage with what's there. Set up the following stations:

1. Think
Set out photocopies of the "Who Made…" quiz (p. 166-167) with some pens or pencils. Write "Answers" on an envelope, and put the copied answer sheet inside. Set out a small trash can for teenagers to throw away their finished quizzes.

2. Make
Set out several large lumps of modeling dough and one or more plastic trays or place mats that teenagers can put their finished models on. Write the following instructions on a piece of paper to set near the modeling dough, and make one sample creature yourself to place by the instructions:

"The world is full of strange and wonderful creatures. Now you have a chance to make your own. Design an animal that can both swim and walk on land, that's smaller than a horse and that eats carrots."

(If you don't have access to modeling dough, set out paper, crayons, and a card with written instructions that prompt them to draw creatures.)

3. Play

Set out plastic building blocks and some instruction sheets for making various models. Don't set out any other instructions—just allow them to use the blocks and see what they can make. Some teenagers may follow the instruction sheets, while others may just do their own thing.

(If you don't have access to plastic building blocks and instruction sheets, set out several square sheets of paper and instructions for making origami. You could borrow an origami book from the library or search for instructions on the Internet. There are multiple sites with directions for making simple origami models.)

4. Watch (optional)

Set up a TV and DVD player, and show footage from a movie that depicts nature, such as the Discovery Channel/BBC series "Planet Earth" (available at most movie rental stores) or other films from PBS, the Discovery Channel, or National Geographic. Select a 20-minute segment to show with the sound muted; be sure to preview it so as not to include scenes that depict mating or predatory behaviors.

Set out a large sheet of butcher paper or white poster board and some markers. At the top, write: "What things in the world around you make you go 'Wow!'?"

Add one or two answers of your own to the butcher paper to spark student responses.

Show DVD to whole group, then journal.

This is an optional station. If you are unable to locate a good video or don't have time to set up a TV and DVD player, simply set up stations 1-3, and skip this final station.

In addition to setting up the stations, prepare a card-stock photocopy of the "Relationship Cross" (p. 169), and cut it out. Also prepare copies of the "Source" take-home handout (p. 154), one section per student.

Take some time to personally engage with the theme of this study by using the Scripture reflection suggestions below.

Engage

Before the study, set aside some time and space for you to reflect on and engage with the story on a personal level.

Read the Creation story in Genesis 1:1–2:3. Read it slowly, allowing a picture of Creation to build up in your mind.

Then take some time to think about each element of creation that's listed below and cultivate an inner sense of wonder. Think of one aspect of that element that makes you go "Wow!" For example, the invention of movies that came from the properties of light for Day 1, the beauty and majesty of a sunrise for Day 4, or the uniqueness of a giraffe for Day 6. Jot down your ideas in a journal, and doodle some pictures if you want. Then spend time praising God for each item you wrote about.

> Day 1: Light
> Day 2: Sky
> Day 3: Land and plants
> Day 4: Sun, moon, and stars
> Day 5: Creatures that swim and fly
> Day 6: Animals, human beings

Pray for your group:

Pray that your group would be open to the wonder and beauty of creation and will see God's fingerprints all over it.

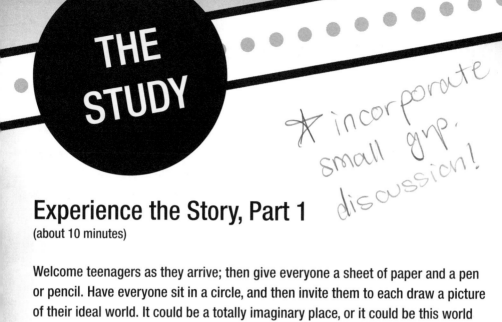

THE STUDY

incorporate small grp. discussion!

Experience the Story, Part 1
(about 10 minutes)

Welcome teenagers as they arrive; then give everyone a sheet of paper and a pen or pencil. Have everyone sit in a circle, and then invite them to each draw a picture of their ideal world. It could be a totally imaginary place, or it could be this world transformed—anything they think of when they hear the phrase "ideal world." After just two minutes, tell teenagers to pass their papers to the people on their left. They should then continue drawing on their new pictures. They can build on what the first person started or can impose their own ideas on the drawing.

Allow teenagers to draw for another two minutes; then ask them to pass their papers again.

Allow a final two minutes for drawing, and then let everyone look at one another's pictures. Have everyone reclaim the drawing he or she started and examine it. Use these questions to discuss the experience together:

- How did you feel about having to hand your picture to someone else? Why?

- What did others do to your picture? Did they ruin it, improve it, or simply change it? Explain.

- How did you treat other people's pictures? Did you build upon what they had drawn or did you impose your own ideas on the pictures?

Tell the group that later on in the study you'll discuss this experience a bit more.

Experience the Story, Part 2
(about 20 minutes)

Draw everyone's attention to the three (or four) stations you've set up around the room. Explain that they've got 20 minutes to explore the stations and do the activities at each one. Let them know they can visit the stations as they'd like—they can aim to visit all three (or four) or could spend extended time at just one or two stations. They can also go to the stations in any order they want. (If your teenagers aren't used to these types of activities or may not follow the printed instructions at the stations, give them a quick overview of each station's activity.)

When everyone understands the basic idea, put on some background music, and have everyone get started. Give the group a warning when there are just five minutes left and again when there are two minutes left.

- *Instead → whole grp DVD & journal*

Tell the Story
(about 15 minutes)

Have everybody gather back together, and invite teenagers to share their feedback on the stations. Which did they like best? What common themes stood out to them as they did the various activities?

Summarize their observations, and then say something like: *The theme of this session is creation. You saw images of things in creation, you tried to identify creators by thinking about what they created, and you had a chance to create your own things using modeling dough and building blocks.* Then tell the group that the Bible starts with the story of God creating this world we live.

TIP

You may want to let teenagers know that there's disagreement among committed, sincere Christians about how God created the world—about whether the description in Genesis is speaking of Creation in a literal seven-day period or whether those days are poetic symbols and the world evolved over time under God's direction. The important point to emphasize is that the Bible says God deliberately designed this world as a place for us to live in.

Small group

Help teenagers form groups of three to five and read Genesis 1:1-5 together. Invite them to skim the rest of the chapter together in their small groups, being sure to read Genesis 1:31–2:3 aloud to wrap up. Invite them to take a few minutes to talk with each other about what they observe in the passage. What are the key events described here? What ideas seem most important?

After about five minutes, have everyone gather back together, and invite volunteers from each small group to share some of their group's observations. Allow about five minutes for teenagers to share their observations, and then affirm and summarize what they've shared. Next, take a few minutes to teach a bit from the passage, being sure to highlight these important points:

- The world is an amazing place full of rich diversity, with just the right conditions to sustain life. Everything that God made is good.

- The world shows us what God is like. Just as teenagers could tell in the quiz who the creator was, so this world has God's fingerprints all over it.

- God gave the world to people to look after. God created us in his image, with the ability to be creative like him. It's our job to develop the raw materials of creation, to unlock its potential, to be inventors. God wants us to do that in a way that pleases him. But that's a risk he has taken, to put the world in our hands.

At the beginning of the study, teenagers placed their drawings in someone else's hands. Some of the results were good; some were frustrating. God took a similar risk in giving us the world to develop. (Draw teenagers' attention to Genesis 1:26-28.)

- God created the world as the place for us to have rich and satisfying relationships.

Use the card-stock Relationship Cross to continue teaching. Hold it up, pointing out each arm of the cross and explaining what it means. Explain that:

- God made us for a relationship with himself. As our creator God loves us deeply.

29

- God made us to have relationships with other people. God made us to live in families and communities, to work together to develop the earth.

- God made us to be at peace with ourselves—to accept and love ourselves.

- God made us to care for the planet so that it can supply all we need.

TIP You'll use the Relationship Cross again in Study 3 and Study 9, so be sure to keep track of it in the weeks to come.

Connect the Story
(about 10 minutes)

Say something like: *As we said last week, we are exploring the big story of the Bible and how it relates to us.* Hold up the "Source" poster. *Each week we're going to create a page of that story together. The Bible starts with the story of Creation, with God creating a beautiful, amazing world to be a stage for the story. God is the source of all life—everything in our universe was ultimately made by him.*

Have participants number off one through six and explain that they each are going to add something to the poster—either a word, symbol, or doodled cartoon. The Ones should write or draw something to symbolize Day 1 of Creation, and the Twos should write or draw something to symbolize Day 2 of Creation, and so on. Invite everyone to crowd around the poster and write or draw something in a blank space.

TIP If you've got more than 15 teenagers, and it's too hard for everyone to gather around the poster at once, have teenagers come up in groups of five to ten, giving each group just one minute to quickly write or scribble a picture.

30

When everyone's done, hold up the poster for all to see.

(Keep this poster for Study 12.)

Respond to the Story
(about 5 minutes)

Invite the group to spend a few minutes thinking about what they have heard during this session. Encourage them to find a space where they are comfortable; if they want, they can lie back and close their eyes. Play some instrumental music in the background to help teenagers relax.

Once everyone is quiet and calm, slowly read the following script to prompt prayerful reflection.

Change to small grp. discuss.

> *The Bible starts like this:*
>
> *"In the beginning God created the heavens and the earth..."*
>
> *That raises loads of questions like: How did he do it? How long did it take? What about the Big Bang and evolution? Questions like these need some thought.*
>
> *But put those questions aside for a moment, and think about some others.*
>
> *If God created the world, why do you think he did it?*
>
> *If God created the world, that means he created you. He designed our complex bodies to grow and develop, to repair themselves when they are hurt, to work hard.*
>
> *Look at your hand for a moment and move your fingers. Think of all the muscles, ligaments, and tendons involved in that movement, almost without you thinking about it. Think of the blood circulating in your veins and the nerves that enable you to feel. Think of the tiny cells that make up your body, the building blocks of life.*

God also created the parts of you that you can't see: your gifts and talents, your determination and passion, your personality and sense of humor. The real you deep inside.

And God loves every part of his creation; God loves you. God looks at you and sees what he has made and says that it's very good.

A poet once said,

You "knit me together in my mother's womb.

Thank you for making me so wonderfully complex!

Your workmanship is marvelous—how well I know it."

Spend a moment thanking God for creating you.

Think about the potential you have to live life to the full, to create, to explore, to be involved in this beautiful world.

What do you want to say to God? This is your chance.

Allow a moment of quietness after you're done reading, and then invite everyone to open their eyes, sit up, and bring their attention back to the room.

Pass out the "Source" take-home handouts, one per student. Remind everyone to set aside about 15 minutes (or more) during the week to explore the story more deeply on their own using the handout. Explain that they each can tape the handout into a notebook that can serve as an exploration journal throughout the series. They can use their exploration journals as their own personal space for writing down their questions and thoughts.

Key Passage

"Then God looked over all he had made, and he saw that it was very good! And evening passed and morning came, marking the sixth day. So the creation of the heavens and the earth and everything in them was completed."

- Genesis 1:31–2:1

This Key Passage can help teenagers grasp the main idea of the study. You can use it in different ways, such as

- writing it on a poster and hanging the poster up in your meeting space,

- projecting it on a screen,

- inviting teenagers to write it on blank business cards that they can keep in their wallets or pockets,

- prompting teenagers to write it on sticky notes and stick the notes on their mirrors or nightstands at home, or

- challenging teenagers to memorize it on their own during the week.

3 BROKEN

Aims

This study will help teenagers

- understand the scope of the Fall and its implications for our relationships with God, with ourselves, with others, and with creation.

- catch a glimpse of God's intention to put things right.

Key Passage

"We are made right with God by placing our faith in Jesus Christ. And this is true for everyone who believes, no matter who we are. For everyone has sinned; we all fall short of God's glorious standard. Yet God, with undeserved kindness, declares that we are righteous. He did this through Christ Jesus when he freed us from the penalty for our sins."

- Romans 3:22-24

Overview

Experience the Story	20 minutes	Teenagers will work together to carry out a task, but each of them will have to do so with some sort of barrier, making it tougher.
Tell the Story/Connect the Story	20 minutes	Teenagers will learn about the Fall, discovering that the first people disobeyed God and every good part of God's creation was spoiled and broken.
Respond to the Story	20 minutes	Teenagers will express their personal responses to the Fall through writing or creating art with partners.

Supplies

Make sure you've got
- ❑ Bibles
- ❑ paper and pens
- ❑ for each team of 4 teenagers, you'll need: 1 set of earplugs, 1 blindfold, and 1 photocopy of "Top Critics" handout (p. 170)
- ❑ card-stock Relationship Cross used in Study 2 (also on p. 169)
- ❑ 1 large blank piece of poster board (Keep this poster for the final study.)
- ❑ 1 black marker
- ❑ variety of paper and art supplies for individual student projects, such as pieces of card stock, acrylic or tempera paint, watercolor paint, paintbrushes, magazines, scissors, glue, colored pencils, crayons, construction paper, scraps of fabric, magazines, craft sticks
- ❑ newspaper or plastic tarps

❑ iPod or CD player with music for the Respond to the Story activity. If you can, select songs (sacred or secular) that connote anger, brokenness, or darkness. Or, play some of your group's favorite songs that have a rock, punk, or alternative feel.

❑ photocopies of "Broken" take-home handout (p. 155), cut apart, 1 per student

Before the Study

Designate a part of your room for the art projects at the end of this study, and lay out some newspaper or tarps on the floor to protect it from accidental spills. Set out the various art supplies in that area. Also, prepare copies of the "Broken" take-home handout (p. 155), one per student.

Take some time to personally engage with the theme of this study by using the Scripture reflection suggestions below.

Engage

Before the study, set aside some time and space for you to reflect on and engage with the story on a personal level.

Read Genesis 3:1-24. Imagine the drama of this event and the ripples that spread from it through all creation. Now think about your experience of sin and brokenness and how it has affected

- your relationship with God.
- your relationships with others.
- your relationship with yourself.
- your relationship with creation.

Spend some time talking to God, crying out for his healing and restoration in these areas. Write down one hope you have for each of these areas, and invite God to bring his healing.

Pray for your group:
Pray that they would be able to see the reality of how sin has affected our world and how God feels about it, but that they also would have a sense of expectation about God's determination to put things right.

Experience the Story

(about 20 minutes)

Welcome everyone as they arrive and then help teenagers form teams of four. Tell them you want each team to imagine they're a group of top film critics—they're going to prepare a one to two-minute film review as a team and then present it to the rest of the group. They can select any movie they want as long as it is one every member of their team has seen. In their reviews, teams should tell the story of the film—without giving away any plot spoilers, highlight what they liked about it, and what they felt didn't work. Emphasize that each person in the team *must* take part in the presentation to the large group.

 If teams can't think of a movie they have all seen, they could do a TV show, a music album, or even a video game.

Once everyone has got the basic idea of the task before them, explain this twist: Every person will communicate through some kind of barrier. One person in each group will be blindfolded. One person will wear earplugs. One person will speak a foreign language all the time. One person will not speak but can only communicate in writing.

After the moaning and groaning, stress again that everyone must take part in the presentation, even if it is only a small part.

Pass out a copy of the "Top Critics" handout, a set of earplugs, paper and pens, and a blindfold to each team, and give them just one minute to decide who will have which communication barrier. When one minute is up, have them start working.

Allow teams about eight minutes to come up with their movie reviews. During that time, walk around the room and help the groups as they attempt to prepare. Make sure teenagers are sticking with the communication barriers they have been given!

There will likely be a fair amount of frustration among teenagers as they attempt to work, so be ready to suggest ways in which they can all take part in the presentation. For example, the person who can't speak could write subtitles or headings for the review and hold them up in the appropriate places. Someone speaking only French could say "oui" whenever the presentation needs a "we"— for example:

> French speaker: Oui…

> Blindfolded person: …want to tell you about our favorite film

> Nonspeaking person: (holds up board with title of film)

> Earplugged person: (reads out title)

Let teams know when they have two minutes of prep time left. Then, when time's up, call Top Critic teams up, one at a time, to present their reviews to each other. Lead everyone else in applauding after each review, affirming teenagers for their creativity and inventiveness.

TIP

If you're doing this study with a large number of teenagers, assign three or four teams to get together and present their film reviews to one another rather than having each team of four present its film review to the entire group.

Tell the Story/Connect the Story
(about 20 minutes)

Invite everyone to share their feedback on the last activity. Ask:

- How did you feel during this experience? Why?

- How did you try to overcome the communication barriers?

- Be honest: Did any of you cheat? Why or why not?

- Did you get used to having to communicate with barriers? Or was it tough the whole time? Explain.

Summarize teenagers' feedback and then begin teaching about the Fall. Say something like:

In the last session we talked about the perfect world that God created. But it's not perfect at the moment is it? Around us we see war, poverty, terrorism, and disease alongside beauty and order. Inside us we see jealousy, sorrow, guilt, and hatred alongside love, acceptance, and friendship. So what went wrong?

When God created the first people, Adam and Eve, he placed them in a beautiful garden and told them they could do whatever they wanted except for one thing. And that was that they must never eat from just one tree in the garden. That was the only restriction in the whole of the creation. And it was a restriction for their own protection. God is good and wanted the best for the people he had made. But into this paradise came the voice of temptation.

Invite a volunteer to read Genesis 3:1-5 aloud while everyone else reads along in his or her own Bible.

Then take a few minutes to teach a bit from the passage, being sure to highlight these important points:

- The serpent is Satan, God's enemy, in the form of a creature. Satan gets Adam and Eve to doubt that God is good. They listen to him and decide to disobey God.

- They ate a fruit from the forbidden tree, and in that moment every part of God's creation was spoiled. It was like an electric shock running through the whole of creation. This event is called the Fall by Christians.

Invite another student to read aloud Genesis 3:6-13 while everyone else reads along in his or her own Bible. Then continue to teach from the passage, touching on this key idea:

- Adam and Eve had to leave the garden. They had been used to walking with God in the garden. Now they had to be thrown out of God's presence because God is so perfect. God still loved them deeply, but he could no longer talk with them face to face.

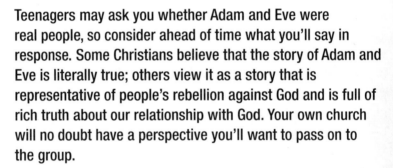

TIP

Teenagers may ask you whether Adam and Eve were real people, so consider ahead of time what you'll say in response. Some Christians believe that the story of Adam and Eve is literally true; others view it as a story that is representative of people's rebellion against God and is full of rich truth about our relationship with God. Your own church will no doubt have a perspective you'll want to pass on to the group.

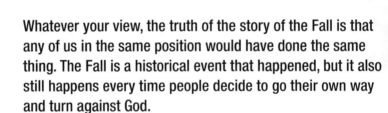

Whatever your view, the truth of the story of the Fall is that any of us in the same position would have done the same thing. The Fall is a historical event that happened, but it also still happens every time people decide to go their own way and turn against God.

Then say something like: *Adam and Eve's actions didn't just affect them; they changed things for us, too.*

Hold up the Relationship Cross from Study 2. *Think back to these rich relationships that God intended us to have. How do you think they have been changed by the Fall?* Divide the group into four subgroups, and assign each subgroup one of the following questions:

1. How did the Fall change our relationship with God?
2. How did the Fall change our relationships with others?

3. How did the Fall change our relationship with ourselves?

4. How did the Fall change our relationship with creation?

Allow three to five minutes for subgroups to discuss their question and brainstorm various effects of the Fall on their given area. Then have everyone gather back together, and hold up the Relationship Cross as you invite the first group to share their ideas about how the Fall changed humanity's relationship with God. As they share, twist the "God" arm of the cross. Be careful not to completely tear it but twist it enough so that it is ruined.

Invite the rest of the group to add any more effects that come to mind for the relationship with God category, and then build upon their suggestions by adding your own ideas.

Continue this pattern of subgroup sharing, large group brainstorming, and twisting the arms of the cross.

Be sure the following concepts are covered during the discussion:

1. **Relationship with God:** Lots of people have no knowledge of God; it can seem hard to connect with God; it can feel hard to see what God is doing in the world; people often experience doubts about God's existence.

2. **Relationships with others:** There's a lot of love in the world but also lots of hatred and distrust exhibited in racism, sexism, torture, wars, and so on.

3. **Relationship with ourselves:** Instead of being confident about being made in God's image, people often doubt themselves, worry, and are afraid; others have forgotten about God entirely and think they are the center of the universe and live as though they have the right to do anything they want.

4. **Relationship with creation:** Instead of caring for the earth in the way that God would have done, we have exploited earth's resources, grabbing what we can for ourselves and polluting the planet.

Hold up the poster board, and invite a volunteer to write the word "Broken" vertically along the left-hand side. Then continue teaching by saying something like:

The ripples of those first people's rebellion spread and touched every part of creation. We live in a fallen, broken world where things are not as God originally intended them to be.

Invite another volunteer to come up and rip the poster board in half vertically. Then hold up just the half that reads "Broken." Say something like: *We can still see the good that God planned, but we can also see how it has been ruined. The Bible calls the brokenness in the world sin.*

And it's hard work living in a broken world. In your movie review experience, you tried to communicate through the barriers, and it took a lot of effort and energy. You managed it, but it wasn't anywhere near as good as what you could have done if you'd been free to be yourselves.

That's what life is like in a broken world. We manage, but it's a pale reflection of what God originally intended for us. We're cut off from God. We're separated from one another. We're discontented with ourselves. And we're abusing the planet.

Tell the group that the torn "Broken" poster will be your page for the big story from this study. Explain to the group that so far in the first three studies you've only covered the first three chapters of the first book of the Bible: Genesis. Write a big letter G somewhere on the "Broken" poster to indicate the small slice of Scripture you've covered. But tell teenagers not to worry—you'll cover much more than three chapters in each of the next sessions!

(Keep the poster for Study 12.)

 TIP You'll use the Relationship Cross again in Study 9, so be sure to keep track of it in the weeks to come.

Respond to the Story
(about 20 minutes)

Say something like: *So far the big story of the Bible has been pretty discouraging. In the next few weeks, we'll look at what God did to put things right, but for now I want you to think about how that brokenness has affected you, your friends and family, and the world you live in.*

Have participants form pairs with whomever they'd like, and point out the art supplies you've set out. Challenge them to take the next twenty minutes to work with their partners to make something that expresses how the Fall has affected relationships across creation. The sky's the limit: They could write a poem or song lyrics, paint or draw a picture, create a cartoon storyboard, make a collage, build something, or come up with something totally out of the box.

Turn on the background music you've prepared, and allow this final part of the study to be free and open as teenagers do their own thing. Some may be serious and intent; others may be talking and having a good time while they work—and that's fine as long as they are making something that expresses their thoughts or ideas.

Tell everyone when ten minutes have passed and again when there are five minutes left. As teenagers finish their work, invite them to look at what others are making.

Wrap up with a short prayer. Ask everyone to leave their art with you; you'll be using it again in Study 11. Then pass out the "Broken" take-home handouts, one per student. Remind teenagers to set aside about 15 minutes (or more) during the week to explore the story more deeply on their own using the handouts. Explain that they each can tape the handout into a notebook that can serve as an exploration journal throughout the series. They can use their exploration journals as their own personal space for writing down their questions and thoughts.

Key Passage

"We are made right with God by placing our faith in Jesus Christ. And this is true for everyone who believes, no matter who we are. For everyone has sinned; we all fall short of God's glorious standard. Yet God, with undeserved kindness, declares that we are righteous. He did this through Christ Jesus when he freed us from the penalty for our sins."

- Romans 3:22-24

This key passage can help teenagers grasp the main idea of the study. You can use it in different ways, such as

- writing it on a poster and hanging the poster up in your meeting space,

- projecting it on a screen,

- inviting teenagers to write it on blank business cards that they can keep in their wallets or pockets,

- prompting teenagers to write it on sticky notes and stick the notes on their mirrors or nightstands at home, or

- challenging teenagers to memorize it on their own during the week.

INVITATION

4

Aims

This study will help teenagers

- learn about God's intention to restore his relationship with people as shown in the story of the people of Israel.

- come to appreciate the calling God gave to Israel: They were blessed to be a blessing.

Key Passage

The Lord had said to Abram, "I will make you into a great nation. I will bless you and make you famous, and you will be a blessing to others. I will bless those who bless you and curse those who treat you with contempt. All the families on earth will be blessed through you."

- Genesis 12:1-3

Overview

Experience the Story	20 minutes	Teenagers will try to reassemble torn up posters to discover how difficult it is to make something like new. Also, a few teenagers will be selected for a special privilege—eating cake—but will then have to clean up afterward to experience both the privilege and responsibility of being chosen.
Tell the Story	10 minutes	Teenagers will learn that God was determined to put right what had been broken in the Fall and invited the people of Israel into a relationship with himself.
Connect the Story	5 minutes	Teenagers will reassemble a torn poster.
Respond to the Story	25 minutes	Teenagers will hold an Ideas Exhibition, exploring how the world, their community, and themselves would be different if they lived by the Ten Commandments

Supplies

Make sure you've got
- ❏ Bibles
- ❏ pens, pencils, and markers
- ❏ adult volunteer
- ❏ several large pop-culture posters (movie and band, for example). You'll need about 1 poster for every 2 to 3 teenagers. (These posters will be ruined, so purchase cheap ones.)
- ❏ large paper or plastic bag
- ❏ several rolls of various kinds of tape (duct, transparent, masking). You'll need about one roll for about every 5 teenagers.
- ❏ delicious cake or brownies (homemade, if possible) - enough for 1 piece per student

- plates, napkins, and silverware (or plastic ware)
- dirtied bowl and cooking supplies from making the cake or brownies—with ample batter caked on the bowl, whisk, measuring cups, etc. (If possible, include more messy, dirtied supplies than you actually used!)
- dish soap, sponges, dish towels
- sink for washing dishes
- photocopies of "The Ten Commandments" handout (p. 171), 1 per student
- 1 large blank piece of poster board (Keep this poster for the final study.)
- 3 large sheets of butcher paper or flip-chart paper
- red, yellow, and green sticky dots
- tape
- photocopies of the "Invitation" take-home handout (p. 155), cut apart, 1 per student

Before the Study

Buy some inexpensive pop-culture posters for the opening activity. Some can be of celebrities or bands your group likes; others can be exceptionally cheesy, like preteen idols, boy bands, and 80s glam rock bands. If you can, try to get a variety of types of posters. Then tear up each poster into about 20 to 30 pieces. Be sure to make a few very jagged tears that will be nearly impossible to mend with tape and also try to tear off just a few tiny shreds and throw them away. When the posters are torn up, put the pieces into a bag.

You also need to make a delicious cake or brownies for this session—the more delicious the better. You will need enough for each member of the group to have a piece, so if you have a large group you may need two cakes. If cooking isn't your strong point, enlist the help of someone at your church. Be sure that whoever makes the dessert leaves the mixing bowl, whisk, and other cooking supplies very messy with caked-on batter. Keep the cake hidden away, and set the messy cooking supplies, dish soap, sponges, and towels in a kitchen (or bathroom with sink) near your meeting room.

During the Experience the Story section of this study, you'll have two groups of teenagers in two different areas doing tasks or discussing things. It will be best if you have at least one adult volunteer ready to go with one of the groups, oversee its activity, and lead its discussion time. (See page 54 for the discussion questions, and have the volunteer look over them ahead of time.)

Write each of these questions at the top of a sheet of butcher paper:

- What would the world be like if people lived by the Ten Commandments?

- What would your school be like if people lived by the Ten Commandments?

- What would you be like if you lived by the Ten Commandments?

Prepare your Connect the Story poster board by writing the word "Invitation" in large letters at the top. Below that, in slightly smaller letters, write the word "Law." Then, in smaller letters, write the first five books of the Bible scattered around on the poster: Genesis, Exodus, Leviticus, Numbers, and Deuteronomy. Last, make your poster into a puzzle of sorts by tearing it into five to eight large, odd-shaped pieces. Collect the pieces, and keep them together for Connect the Story.

Prepare photocopies of "The Ten Commandments" (p. 171) and "Invitation" (p. 155).

Take some time to personally engage with the theme of this study by using the Scripture reflection suggestions below.

Engage

Before the study, set aside some time and space for you to reflect on and engage with the story on a personal level.

Read Genesis 12:1-5, where God calls Abram—the genesis of his chosen people.

Then read Ephesians 1:3-14. Read slowly, savoring every word. This is a rich passage that contains so much truth it is hard to take it all in. You are part of God's chosen people through what Jesus has accomplished on the cross. You are chosen by God.

Write out the truths in this passage as they apply to you. For example, from verse 3 you could write: "God has blessed me in the heavenly realms with every spiritual blessing in Christ."

Write each truth on a sticky note, and put a fresh note on your fridge door each day. These truths are so life-changing that we need to keep coming back to them.

Thank God for the truth contained in this passage—that he has chosen you, redeemed you, and included you!

Pray for your group:
Think about your group: Who has already responded to God, and who needs to hear his invitation? Pray for each person's need—that he or she would be intrigued by this story, long to be chosen by God, hear God's personal invitation, and respond wholeheartedly.

THE STUDY

Experience the Story

(about 20 minutes)

Welcome teenagers as they arrive, and then dump out the torn poster pieces on the floor in the middle of the room. Pass out the rolls of tape to different teenagers, and ask the group to help you reassemble the posters. Don't tell participants what the pictures on the posters are, but do let them know how many posters total they need to put back together. Tell them to do their best to make the posters look as close as possible to their original condition.

> **TIP**
>
> This 20-minute Experience the Story segment is broken into three parts, so plan accordingly:
>
> Four minutes: Everyone works together to put torn posters back together.
>
> Eight minutes: A majority of the teenagers continue working on the posters while a special chosen group eats cake.
>
> Eight minutes: The poster group now rests, eats dessert, and has a discussion; the chosen group cleans up cooking supplies and has a discussion.

After about four minutes of work, call out the names of a few of the teenagers, and invite them to join you in a corner of the room in full view of everyone else. Pick one-fourth or one-fifth of your group size to be the "chosen few." Try to select teenagers randomly—not based on any obvious traits or behaviors.

Ignore the rest of the group who are working on the posters as you bring out the cake (only enough for this special group). Invite your chosen group to eat the dessert, explaining that you had it made especially for them. Talk to the chosen group about your plans for a new special youth group you'd like them to be part of. Don't be derogatory about any of the people you haven't chosen, but do emphasize the benefits and privileges this new chosen group will have. You could say that you've seen that they have great potential and you want to invest time and energy into getting to know them better; that you might ask for a bigger budget from the church so they can go on outings; that you're planning to take them to some cool events, and so on. Invite them to give you ideas of what they would like to do. If they ask about the others in the group, tell them not to worry about them for now.

Allow the special group to chat and eat for a while. When they have finished the cake (or when about eight minutes have passed), say something like: *Of course when you have special privileges, you also have extra responsibilities, so I'm sure you won't mind washing up the dishes for this cake you've just enjoyed.*

Tell the group working on the posters to take a break, and ask everyone to follow you to the kitchen. Explain that the special group who got to relax and eat cake will now get the responsibility of cleaning up. Give group members dish soap, sponges, and towels, and have them get to work. If they protest, point out that since they have enjoyed the cake, it's only fair that they should take up some responsibilities, too.

Lead the rest of the teenagers back to your main area, and serve them the remaining cake. For the next eight minutes, the larger group will eat in the meeting area while the chosen group will clean. Each group should discuss the experience while they eat or clean. (Have another adult volunteer help you by leading one of the discussions.)

Ask the larger group questions like:

- What was your reaction to the job of putting the posters back together and making them look like new? How successful were you in your efforts to put the posters back together?

- What did you think and feel as you saw others get chosen to have special privileges?

- What do you think now that you see they've also got extra responsibilities?

Ask the chosen group questions like:

- How did it feel to be chosen? What did you think or feel as you ate cake while your friends worked on the posters?

- Why do you think you were chosen?

- What do you think about having to clean up now? Do you think it's fair? Why or why not?

Tell the Story
(about 10 minutes)

Call everyone back together, and take about 10 minutes to explain the link between their experiences and Scripture by teaching them these key biblical points:

- Explain that mending something that's broken is often very difficult. Have teenagers hold up the posters they've been working on. (It's OK if some are unfinished). Even if some of the posters have been taped back together, they probably won't look very good. They aren't the quality of poster someone would want to hang in his or her room! It's impossible to get them back to the state they were in before they were broken.

- Remind teenagers that in the last study you talked about how God's fantastic world was ruined by sin and about the relationships that were broken as a result—between God and us, between each other, within ourselves, and with creation. But God didn't want to leave things that way. God wanted to put things right because he really loved the people he had made. But he couldn't just ignore what had happened or magically make the problem of sin go away. And he didn't want an inadequate, half-done repair job where you could still see the tears and the wrinkles and the parts that were missing. Serious damage had been done to the structure of the world through humanity's disobedience. So God needed a plan to put things completely right again.

- God decided to choose one group of people and invite them back into a relationship with him. He chose a man named Abram to be the father of this group—some of his descendants would be able to have their

54

relationship with God restored. God made a covenant with Abram, a strong promise that God would be with him and would bless him and his faithful descendants.

Have a student volunteer read aloud Genesis 12:1-5 while everyone else follows along in his or her own Bible.

Explain that this was a unique opportunity to be God's special people and to walk closely with God again, a lot like the small group that was chosen to have cake and all the privileges you talked about with them.

- With privilege comes responsibility. Pass out "The Ten Commandments" handout (p. 171), one per student. Then explain that Abraham's descendants came to be known as the people of Israel. Because the people of Israel were God's people, they needed to be like God—to be without sin. None of us are able to live perfect lives, no matter how hard we try. This was true for the people of Israel, too. God knew they couldn't be sinless, so he gave the people laws to show them the standard they needed to live up to, and he also gave them a way of putting things right when they got it wrong.

  The story of this time is found in the first five books of the Bible: Genesis, Exodus, Leviticus, Numbers, and Deuteronomy. The laws God gave his people are summed up in the Ten Commandments. God wanted people to live by these standards, to do their best to put God first, and to make wise decisions in life. But when his people broke any of the laws, they could put things right by making a sacrifice. That's a bit like the way the chosen group in the earlier activity had to wash dishes. They had an extra responsibility that came along with their privilege. Similarly, the people of Israel had responsibilities that came with the privilege of being close to God.

- Choosing a group for a special purpose may seem a bit unfair. After all, what about the people who aren't chosen? It's not a good way to run a youth group—you only did it as an illustration. However, God chose a whole community to have a covenant with rather than just a few people out of a group like you did.

And what God wanted was for the people of Israel to show the rest of the world what he had originally planned for all of them. God wanted the people of Israel to be a living example of the relationship that he had intended for everyone

- to have a close relationship with God;

- to be people living in peace together and looking out for the poor and oppressed in their community;

- to be people who knew they were God's children and what life was all about; and

- to be people who looked after the land responsibly and carefully, making sure it provided enough for everyone.

So the people of Israel weren't supposed to stay in a holy huddle feeling superior; they were supposed to show people what God was like. They had been blessed so that they could be a blessing to other people. They were supposed to share their cake!

Connect the Story
(about 5 minutes)

Hand the torn pieces of the "Invitation" poster you prepared to five to eight teenagers. Give another one or two teenagers rolls of tape. Ask them to come to the front and work together to reassemble the poster. As they do, invite the rest of the group to respond to your teaching in the Tell the Story section. Ask questions like:

- What's your initial reaction to the part of God's big story that I just explained? What stands out to you most? Why?

- Imagine you were Abram. How would you have felt to receive this special invitation from God?

- How would you have felt if you were one of the people of Israel—with a special relationship with God but also with high standards you had to live up to? Explain.

When the poster has been reassembled, hold it up and say something like: *This poster represents the part of God's big story we've talked about today. It will symbolize for us the main idea of the first five books of the Bible: Genesis, Exodus, Leviticus, Numbers, and Deuteronomy. Though there was brokenness in the world caused by sin, God invited his chosen people to have a special relationship with him and to live by his laws.*

Respond to the Story
(about 25 minutes)

Say something like: *Often we view the Ten Commandments as a list of things we can't do. However, if everyone were to live according to the Ten Commandments, there would be huge positive benefits because we would be living as God intended us to.*

Divide your group into three subgroups. Give each group a bunch of pens and one of the three sheets of butcher paper you prepared. Invite each subgroup to read the question on the paper, and then respond to the question by writing down quick thoughts on the paper. Encourage them to read through "The Ten Commandments" handout and use it to guide their brainstorming. After about five minutes, have teenagers stick all three sheets of butcher paper on the wall (with tape or tacks). (If you've got the space, put each sheet of butcher paper on a different wall.)

If you have more than 20 to 30 teenagers, form six subgroups instead of three. Create six newsprint sheets, making two of each question. During the Ideas Exhibition, make sure subgroups look at the two questions that are different than their own.

Tell everyone you're now going to have an Ideas Exhibition. This will be an opportunity for class members to consider others' ideas and compare or contrast them with their own.

Give each subgroup a sheet of red, green, and yellow sticky dots, and ask each subgroup to stand in front of another subgroup's sheet. Together, they should read through the ideas written on the sheet and decide if they generally agree or disagree with each statement. To indicate their opinion about each idea, the subgroup will put a colored dot sticker next to it. They should add a green dot if they agree with what's written, a red dot if they disagree, and a yellow dot if they are unsure. Participants can also add their own ideas to the bottom of the sheets, but they cannot restate something that has already been said.

After about five minutes, have subgroups move to the next sheet and do the same thing.

When about five more minutes have passed, have subgroups take down their original sheets of butcher paper and look at what's been written there and marked with dots. Invite teenagers to add dots to any new ideas that have been added on their sheets.

Invite the group to share their general reaction to this exercise, asking:

- Some people view rules negatively as restrictions on their freedom. Based on our Ideas Exhibition, what do you see as the positive or negative aspects of living by the Ten Commandments?

- Which of these laws do you think are most difficult for people to live out? Why?

- What benefits of living by God's laws stand out to you most? Why?

Summarize the key ideas they shared or wrote on the posters, and add your own perspective as group leader, pointing out how the benefits of living in God's ways far outweigh the restrictions.

Wrap up your meeting by saying something like: *A world where everyone lived by the Ten Commandments would be pretty close to the paradise God had originally intended the world to be. But that's only possible where people are in relationship with God and receive wisdom and strength from him. This was God's invitation to the people of Israel: to recapture what had been lost in the Fall. But would they accept the invitation? Get ready to find out in the next session.*

Pass out the "Invitation" take-home handouts, one per student. Remind everyone to set aside 15 minutes (or more) during the week to explore the story more deeply on his or her own using the handout. Explain that they can tape the handout into a notebook that can serve as their exploration journal throughout the series. They can use their exploration journals as their own personal space for writing down their questions and thoughts.

Key Passage

"The Lord had said to Abram, "I will make you into a great nation. I will bless you and make you famous, and you will be a blessing to others. I will bless those who bless you and curse those who treat you with contempt. All the families on earth will be blessed through you."

- Genesis 12:1-3

This Key Passage can help teenagers grasp the main idea of the study. You can use it in different ways, such as

- writing it on a poster and hanging the poster up in your meeting space,

- projecting it on a screen,

- inviting teenagers to write it on blank business cards that they can keep in their wallets or pockets,

- prompting teenagers to write it on sticky notes and stick the notes on their mirrors or nightstands at home, or

- challenging teenagers to memorize it on their own during the week.

Aims

This study will help teenagers

- learn that Israel asked for a king, to be like the nations around them, and the consequences of their choice.

- explore the issue of idolatry and its relevance throughout history.

Key Passage

"You must not have any other god but me. You must not make for yourself an idol of any kind or an image of anything in the heavens or on the earth or in the sea. You must now bow down to them or worship them, for I, the Lord your God, am a jealous God who will not tolerate your affection for any other gods."

—Exodus 20:3-5a

Overview

Experience the Story	20 minutes	Teenagers will exercise while leaders try to tempt and distract them.
Tell the Story	15 minutes	The group will learn about the kings of the Old Testament and Israel's and Judah's problems with idolatry.
Respond to the Story, Part 1	10 minutes	Small groups will discuss modern idols.
Respond to the Story, Part 2	10 minutes	Teenagers will create a graffiti wall to represent the idols in our culture.
Connect the Story	5 minutes	Teenagers will pray after considering the theme of this part of God's big story.

Supplies

Make sure you've got

- ❏ Bibles
- ❏ paper and pens
- ❏ clock
- ❏ exercise supplies and silly challenge supplies (as needed); for example, an exercise bike, floor mats, rowing machine, Hula-Hoop, jump-ropes, balloons, table tennis table and set, Twister game. See "Before the Study" for details.
- ❏ adult volunteers
- ❏ some tempting items, like ice-cold soda, candy bars, other treats, cell phone, pillow, comfy chair. See "Before the Study" for details.
- ❏ iPod or CD player for upbeat background music as well as instrumental background music
- ❏ photocopy of "Kings (and Queens) of the Bible" handout (p. 172), cut apart
- ❏ paper bag or bowl
- ❏ large sheets of butcher paper
- ❏ tape
- ❏ colored markers (not black)
- ❏ 1 big, black marker

- ❏ 1 large piece of white poster board (Keep this poster for the final study.)
- ❏ photocopies of "Idols Today" handout (p. 174). You'll need 1 copy for every 3 to 4 teenagers.
- ❏ photocopies of "Choice" take-home handout (p. 156), cut apart, 1 per student

Before the Study

During the Experience the Story segment, teenagers will participate in various "athletic" challenges: some will be serious and some will be silly. You'll want to set up five to ten things teenagers can do over a 15-minute time period. You'll need to set up the activities (with any needed supplies) and set out written instructions in each area. See if you can borrow some exercise equipment from church members. Here are some ideas you could choose from:

- Exercise bike. Challenge: Cycle above 100 rpm for three minutes.
- Floor mats. Challenge: Hold the plank position for three minutes.
- Floor mats. Challenge: Do 20 push-ups.
- Against a wall. Challenge: Hold a sitting position against a wall (without a chair) for three minutes.
- Against a wall. Challenge: See how long you can hold a handstand.
- Rowing machine. Challenge: Row at a target rate for three minutes. (You will need to set a target rate dependent on the rowing machine. Ask its owner for advice!)
- Steps. Challenge: Perform the most step-ups in three minutes.
- Hula-Hoop. Challenge: Keep the hoop going for three minutes.
- Jump-rope. Challenge: Skip rope the most times in three minutes.
- Table tennis. Challenge: Volley the table-tennis ball with a partner for two minutes.

- Balloons. Challenge: Tap a balloon so that it stays off the ground for three minutes…using just your elbows!
- Twister: Play a round of Twister with two others for four minutes without falling down.
- Paper. Challenge: Fold a paper airplane, and fly it all the way across the room.
- Rubber ball. Challenge: Bounce the ball as high as you can.
- Basketball. Challenge: Spin the basketball on your finger for one minute.
- No supplies needed. Challenge: Do 40 jumping jacks.
- No supplies needed. Challenge: Have a staring contest with a partner.
- No supplies needed. Challenge: See how long you can hold your breath.

You and other adult volunteers will tempt teenagers to quit exercising during this segment, so prepare some temptations like snacks, drinks, comfy places to sit and rest, and so on.

Cut apart the "Kings (and Queens) of the Bible" handout (p. 172), and put the pieces in a paper bag or bowl.

Also, prepare photocopies of "Idols Today" (p. 174) and "Choice" (p. 156).

Take some time to personally engage with the theme of this study by using the Scripture reflection suggestions below.

(E)ngage

Before the study, set aside some time and space for you to reflect on and engage with the story on a personal level.

Read Joshua 24:14-27. These are Joshua's words to the Israelites when they have entered the Promised Land. He reminds them that they have to make a choice about whom they will serve.

Then read Matthew 6:19-24 where Jesus presents us with the same choice and names one of the biggest idols of our time. Will we serve God or money?

Get out some money, and place it in front of you next to your Bible as you consider this choice. Talk to God about your decision, and ask God to show you anything that rivals the place that God should have in your life.

Pray for your group:
Pray for God to open their eyes to the reality of false idols in our world. Pray that they would choose to serve the Lord.

THE STUDY

Experience the Story
(about 20 minutes)

Welcome everyone as they arrive, and immediately point out the various athletic activities you've set up in the meeting space. Challenge teenagers to form pairs or trios and try out the various challenges together, with partners keeping track of time or counting for each other. Give them paper and pens, and invite them to write down their achievements as they move through the various challenges. Explain that they've got 15 minutes to do as many challenges as they can, moving on to the next one once each person in their group has completed the one they are on.

Play some upbeat background music to motivate everyone as they exercise. Once they get started, your job—and the job of your other adult volunteers—is to try to distract the teenagers and tempt them to stop the activities they are doing. You could tempt them by

- offering them treats like brownies or candy bars.

- distracting the people who are timing or counting so they lose count and have to start over.

- offering drinks.

- pretending you have a picture on your mobile phone of a celebrity you spotted.

Give everyone a warning after about 10 minutes. When the full 15 minutes have passed, call everyone back together, and get some feedback on the activity. Ask the group:

- Who was able to keep going in spite of the temptations and distractions? Why?

- How did you feel about the people doing the tempting?

- Did anyone give up on the activity because of the distractions or temptations? Why?

Tell the Story
(about 15 minutes)

Invite the group to recap the big story of the Bible so far (based on weeks one through four). If they need help, ask questions to draw out these key ideas:

- God created a beautiful world for people to live in.

- People disobeyed God and the world was spoiled and broken.

- God wanted to put things right—not just put a bandage on the problem— a true restoration to how they were before the Fall.

- God entered into an agreement (covenant) with the people of Israel. They were to be a model of what it was like to live in God's ways, and in return they would live under God's blessing.

Build upon the idea of sin and the law to explain the sacrifices that the Israelites needed to make for sin. Say something like: The Israelites were only human. God knew that they would make mistakes and would fail to keep his laws. So God set up a way that the Israelites could put things right when they did something wrong. As we talked about before, things that are broken are hard to mend. But one way to undo the effects of sin was for blood to be shed. So as part of their worship, the Israelites would get their priests to make a sacrifice in the temple. The priests would kill a lamb, or bull, or pigeon as a way of putting right the sin of the people. Every day, animals would be sacrificed in the temple and other offerings made to make the people right with God again.

Now introduce the kings and the theme of idolatry by saying something like: *The Israelites ended up in the Promised Land, a land of their own where they could live in God's ways. At the beginning they were ruled by people who were called the judges, but later the Israelites asked for a king so they could be like the nations around them. So God gave them a series of kings.*

Explain that the first king was Saul, the next king was David, and the third king was Solomon, David's son. Explain that after Solomon's reign, the nation split into two kingdoms. The northern kingdom kept the name Israel, while the southern kingdom was called Judah.

Pass around the paper bag or bowl with descriptions of the kings who followed Solomon. Tell teenagers how many slips they should draw out. There are 39 slips, so divide that by the number of participants you have so that every slip is drawn.

TIP If you have more than 39 teenagers, have ones without a slip pair up with someone who has.

Have teenagers read what's written on their slips, and then ask them to raise their hands if they're holding the name of a "good" king. (If they've got two good kings, they should raise both hands.) Have them put their hands down. Then ask teenagers to raise their hands if they're holding the name of an "evil" king. (Again, if they've got two evil kings, they should raise both hands.) Have teenagers put their hands down again. Point out that only 9 of the 39 rulers who followed Saul, David, and Solomon were "good" kings—the rest were evil.

Continue teaching by saying something like: *What the people of Israel needed to do was serve God—to follow the guidelines God had given them and to enjoy God's blessing so they could show everyone around them the benefits of being God's people. Sadly, the kings and the people kept getting distracted from this task and tempted away from it—a bit like you did during the athletic activities. Some of you managed to stay focused and resist temptation. You ignored the distractions and completed what you had set out to do. But the Israelites were not so focused. They kept forgetting they were God's people, and they started worshipping the idols and gods of the nations around them.*

Invite a student volunteer to read aloud 1 Kings 14:21-24 while everyone else reads along. Explain that this is typical of the people of Israel and Judah during most of the reigns of the different kings.

Continue teaching by saying something like: *You see everyone at that time worshipped something. People in the other nations created their own idols—statues of a person or a thing—that they set up and worshipped. They offered sacrifices to their idol, prayed to it, and expected the idol to repay their worship with health, wealth, and prosperity. In spite of having a relationship with the one true God, the Israelites chose to worship these false idols instead. So along with the Temple in Jerusalem, where they were to worship God, they had what were sometimes referred to as "high places"—places set up where they could worship these idols. And most of their kings, instead of setting a good example, set a bad example by serving these idols, too. One king, Jeroboam, even made two statues of golden calves for the people to worship. As you saw earlier, when you raised your hands, a few of the kings were good. They worshipped God and destroyed the high places. But most of them were evil. They ignored God and led the people astray.*

Respond to the Story, Part 1
(about 10 minutes)

Have teenagers form small groups of three to four, and give each group an "Idols Today" handout. Invite them to use the questions there to guide their own discussion. Encourage everyone to participate by sharing their own thoughts, opinions, and ideas with the others in their small groups.

Respond to the Story, Part 2
(about 10 minutes)

Have everyone gather back together, then say something like: *Some people would say that everybody serves something; it's an inbuilt response. Just like your heart keeps beating whether you think about it or not. And your body keeps breathing without you having to make a choice or tell it what to do. We all have to worship something.*

What do you think? What do people worship today? What do they make sacrifices for? What do they expect to bring them rewards?

Play instrumental music in the background as you invite everyone to gather around the graffiti wall you've set up. Ask teenagers to write words and draw pictures that represent the "modern idols" people worship today. Suggest participants include various things they talked about in their small groups. Also challenge them to get personal—to write or draw things that represent idols in their own lives. (A blank piece of poster board is part of the graffiti wall—encourage teenagers to write or draw on it just as they are on the rest of the wall.)

After a few minutes, if you notice that some teenagers are stuck and don't know what to write or draw, ask these questions again to help them think about the issue:

> • What kinds of things do people work really hard for?

> • What do they expect to make them happy and successful in life?

> • What do people make sacrifices for?

When most of them are done, have everyone stand back and look at the entire wall. Emphasize that idolatry is still a major issue today—it's not just a thing of the past or just an issue in the Bible. Remind them that we all have to serve something in life; if it's not God, it will be something else.

Connect the Story
(about 5 minutes)

Stand in front of the poster board on the graffiti wall, and explain that it will serve as the page that tells this part of the big story of God. Use a big black marker to write the word "Choice" at the top, reminding teenagers that it ultimately comes down to the choice God's people face: serve him or serve an idol. Then, in smaller letters, write the word "History" on the poster, and explain that this part of Scripture is contained in the historical books of the Bible: Joshua, Judges, Ruth, 1 and 2 Samuel, 1 and 2 Kings, 1 and 2 Chronicles, Ezra, Nehemiah, and Esther.

Then lead a time of prayer about turning away from idols to worship the one true God. You can use this responsive prayer or simply close with words of your own. If you choose to use this responsive prayer, rehearse this part with your group:

When you say: *But instead of worshipping false idols…*
They respond: **Holy God, we turn to you.**

Prayer

Lord God, we have heard how the Israelites worshipped false gods
made of stone and wood, silver and gold.
But instead of worshipping false idols…
Holy God, we turn to you.

We no longer bow down to statues,
yet we are still tempted to give our allegiance to other things.
But instead of worshipping false idols…
Holy God, we turn to you.

We are tempted by money, by thoughts of a comfortable life.
We're prepared to work hard, to make sacrifices, all for cash in our pockets.
But instead of worshipping false idols…
Holy God, we turn to you.

We are tempted by celebrity, by thoughts of being well-known.
We're prepared to work hard, to make sacrifices, all for our 15 minutes of fame.
But instead of worshipping false idols…
Holy God, we turn to you.

We are tempted by success, by thoughts of having power.
We're prepared to work hard, to make sacrifices, all for our time at the top.
But instead of worshipping false idols…
Holy God, we turn to you.

Holy God, we recognize that these idols can't deliver what they promise.
Only you can give us a place to belong, forgiveness for what we do wrong.
We choose to worship you wholeheartedly,
to serve you every day of our lives,
to put you first.
Instead of worshipping false idols…
Holy God, we turn to you. Amen

Pass out the "Choice" take-home handouts, one per student. Remind everyone to set aside 15 minutes (or more) during the week to explore the story more deeply on his or her own using the handout. Explain that they each can tape the handout into a notebook that can serve as an exploration journal throughout the series. They can use their exploration journals as their own personal space for writing down their questions and thoughts.

After the study, take down the "Choice" poster, and write these books of the Bible on it: Joshua, Judges, Ruth, 1 and 2 Samuel, 1 and 2 Kings, 1 and 2 Chronicles, Ezra, Nehemiah, and Esther.

(Keep the poster for Study 12.)

Key Passage

"You must not have any other god but me. You must not make for yourself an idol of any kind or an image of anything in the heavens or on the earth or in the sea. You must now bow down to them or worship them, for I, the Lord your God, am a jealous God who will not tolerate your affection for any other gods."
- Exodus 20:3-5a

This Key Passage can help teenagers grasp the main idea of the study. You can use it in different ways, such as

- writing it on a poster and hanging the poster up in your meeting space,

- projecting it on a screen,

- inviting teenagers to write it on blank business cards that they can keep in their wallets or pockets,

- prompting teenagers to write it on sticky notes and stick them on their mirrors or nightstands at home, or

- challenging teenagers to memorize it on their own during the week.

REALITY (6)

Aims

This study will help teenagers

- understand that the Bible is relevant to all the key issues we are concerned with: how to live, the meaning of life, sex, friendships, money and so on.

- reflect on and interact with passages from Proverbs and Psalms.

- realize that we can be honest with God about how we feel.

Key Passage

"My victory and honor come from God alone. He is my refuge, a rock where no enemy can reach me. O my people, trust in him at all times. Pour out your heart to him, for God is our refuge."

- Psalm 62:7-8

Overview

Experience the Story, Part 1	15 minutes	Teenagers will explore the various feelings they've experienced over the past week.
Experience the Story, Part 2	15 minutes	Groups will draw on principles from Proverbs to give advice.
Tell the Story	10 minutes	Teenagers will read some psalms and discover the real, honest way psalms portray human emotions.
Connect the Story	5 minutes	Teenagers will create a poster that represents the theme of this week's study.
Respond to the Story	15 minutes	Teenagers will write their own psalms.

Supplies

Make sure you've got

- ❏ Bibles
- ❏ paper, pens, markers
- ❏ 5 different colored pieces of poster board or card stock. Choose four colors that can represent happy, sad, angry, and scared (such as yellow, blue, red, and purple). The fifth poster will be used to represent any other emotions teenagers feel, so choose a color that could represent a variety of feelings, like green, orange, or gray.
- ❏ tape
- ❏ 2 to 3 photocopies of "Shades of Emotions" (p. 175), cut apart. (If you can, use a photocopier to enlarge each quadrant of the page.)
- ❏ photocopies of the "I Need Advice" handout (p. 176), cut apart. You'll need 1 cut-apart section for every 3 teenagers.
- ❏ index cards or slips of paper
- ❏ photocopies of the "Write Your Own Psalm" handout (p. 178), 1 per student
- ❏ 1 large piece of white poster board
- ❏ glue

❑ iPod or CD player for instrumental background music
❑ photocopies of the "Reality" take-home handout (p. 156), cut apart,
1 per student

Before the Study

Write "happy," "sad," "angry," and "scared" at the top of each of the four colored poster boards choosing the most appropriate colors. Leave the fifth poster blank. Hang up each poster in a different area of your meeting space. Photocopy the "Shades of Emotions" handout two or three times, and cut out the four sections on each page. (If you can, use a copy machine to enlarge each section a bit.) Stick a few copies of the appropriate "Shades of Emotions" section on the wall around the corresponding colored poster. Don't hang anything next to the fifth colored poster.

Write each of the following Scripture references on index cards or slips of paper that you'll pass out to volunteer readers:

- Psalm 13
- Psalm 23
- Psalm 37:3-5
- Psalm 51:1-10
- Psalm 55:1-5, 16-17
- Psalm 103:1-5, 8-12

Ready your Connect the Story white poster board by writing the word "Reality" in large letters at the top. In large letters, write the word "Wisdom" near the bottom of the poster. Then in smaller letters, list these books of the Bible near the word "Wisdom": Job, Psalms, Proverbs, Ecclesiastes, Song of Songs. Leave a large blank area in the middle of the poster.

Prepare photocopies of "I Need Advice" (p. 176), "Write Your Own Psalm" (p. 178), and "Reality" (p. 156).

Also take some time to personally engage with the theme of this study by using the Scripture reflection suggestions below.

Engage

Before the study, set aside some time and space for you to reflect on and engage with the story on a personal level.

How do you feel today? Choose one psalm from the list below that best matches your mood. Read it, savor it, and use it as a springboard to express your own feelings to God.

Crying for help: Psalm 38
Delighted in God: Psalm 46
Fearful or worried: Psalm 55
Guilty: Psalm 51
Joyful: Psalm 145 or Psalm 139
Sad: Psalm 42 or Psalm 13

Then, after you've read one, choose a psalm that reflects a mood that's very different from how you're feeling right now. As you read it, think about the language used and the honesty of the emotions expressed.

Consider these questions: How honest are you with God? How able are you to be yourself? Thank God he loves and accepts you no matter how you feel or what you are experiencing.

Pray for your group:
Pray that they would know God's acceptance and love for them deep at the core of who they are. Pray that they would be able to be honest with God about their thoughts and feelings.

Experience the Story, Part 1

(about 15 minutes)

Welcome teenagers as they arrive. When everyone's settled, ask the group:

- How are you feeling?

Invite responses from the group. If no one says anything, call on a few teenagers and ask—for example, "Hey Rob, how are you feeling? How was your week?" or "Christie, how's it going? How are you feeling?"

Most of the teenagers probably won't be very specific.

Say something like: *It's funny, isn't it, that we experience a whole range of emotions, but when people ask us how we're feeling, we usually just say "fine" or "good." I've never heard someone say, "Well, actually, I feel so depressed I don't know what to do anymore" or "I feel really guilty about something I did last week."*

Draw teenagers' attention to the five colored posters on the walls in your meeting space, pointing out the specific emotion they each represent. Explain that there are the four main emotions people feel. Within each one there is a range of depth of feeling represented on the "Shades of Emotions" sheet beside each one. Then point out the fifth poster which is sort of a catchall to represent any other emotions that might not fit under the four big categories.

Invite participants to take a minute or two to think back over the past week and try to identify all the different emotions they have experienced. After about one minute of quietness, use the following prompts to help them think. Teenagers shouldn't answer these questions out loud—they should reflect on them privately. (Be sure to pause for 15 to 30 seconds between each question.) Ask:

- When were you happy this week? What made you feel that way?

- When did you feel sad? What caused those emotions?

- When were you angry this week? What made you feel angry?

- When did you feel scared? What caused you to feel that way?

- What other emotions did you experience? Why?

Now invite everyone to get up, grab a pen or marker, and mingle around the room visiting each of the emotion posters on the walls. Explain that at each poster, each participant should read the "Shades of Emotions" sign near it and select a word that best represents the feeling he or she experienced. Then each participant should write the chosen word on the colored poster. Teenagers should also write any other feelings on the fifth poster that they don't think are covered under the categories happy, sad, angry, and scared.

Allow about five to eight minutes for teenagers to mingle and write words. (If you'd like, play music in the background during this part.)

Then have everyone gather back together again. Walk around the room, and read aloud some of the words written on each poster. If you can, read aloud some mild emotions as well as some of the more extreme ones.

Say something like: *The reality is that as human beings we're often much more than just "fine." We experience great happiness and deep sadness. We face extreme difficulties or harbor hidden fears. There is a vast range of how we feel.*

Thank the group for their willingness to be honest and real in the words they wrote down.

Experience the Story, Part 2
(about 15 minutes)

Explain that sometimes emotions can be quite difficult to deal with, and it often helps to talk them over with a friend. Have teenagers form groups of three, and tell them that each small group is going to imagine they have a website that offers people advice. Pass out paper, pens, and an "I Need Advice" handout section to each trio (being sure to pass out all four different letters). Explain that it's their job to take this letter from a young person seriously and try to compose a reply. Point out that the handout includes some "Helpful Hints"—advice that comes from the Bible. Trios can use that advice in their letters—but they don't have to. It's up to them to decide if they think the Helpful Hints are good advice.

The Helpful Hints below each letter are actual passages of Scripture. If you want, you can encourage teenagers to look them up in their own Bibles, too. Allow about seven minutes for trios to write their replies; then have volunteers from the trios read their letters to the rest of the group.

When all the advice replies have been read, invite the group to discuss the experience, asking it questions like:

- Did you find the Helpful Hints useful? Why or why not?

- When you have questions like this in your own life, who do you turn to? What kind of person do you seek out when you want advice?

Tell the Story
(about 10 minutes)

Reiterate that the Helpful Hints they read were all from the Bible. Explain that though the Bible was written thousands of years ago, it can still speak to us today. Many experiences and emotions we have are found throughout humanity across the centuries, and so wisdom that was relevant then is still helpful today. The Bible is "God-breathed"—inspired by God who is the creator of life and who knows how life is meant to work. So it's not surprising that we'll find help in the Bible for whatever problem in life we are trying to deal with.

Invite teenagers to flip open their Bibles right in the middle. Tell them that the books that are right about in the middle of their Bibles are called the wisdom books. Explain a bit about these books. Say something like: Some of the books of the Bible are called the wisdom books because they give us wisdom for how to live. They're not the only place that wisdom is found in the Bible, but they do give us special insight into life and the nature of reality. The Helpful Hints you read were from the book of Proverbs; other wisdom books are Job, Psalms, Ecclesiastes, and Song of Songs.

Invite the group to look specifically at Psalms for a moment. Say something like: *Psalms is a book of songs, most of which were written by King David. In the psalms you'll find a whole range of emotions: from ecstatic to depressed, from fearful to despairing. They're not polite, nice, sanitized songs. They're often raw and brutally honest. David poured out his heart to God, even when he was angry with God or had difficult questions to ask God. Psalms come from the heart. Let's listen to a few.*

Ask for volunteers to read some passages (or simply select volunteers yourself), and pass out the Scripture references from Psalms you prepared in advance.

Invite readers to stand up as they read their passages aloud, prompting everyone else to read along in his or her own Bible. After each psalm is read, ask group members to quickly and briefly call out the emotions that are directly expressed in it or other emotions they think the writer was feeling when he composed the psalm. The group should be able to identify these feelings and experiences in the passages:

- Psalm 13—feeling helpless and sad
- Psalm 23—feeling safe and secure in God's hands
- Psalm 37:3-5—feelings of delight and trust
- Psalm 51:1-10—feelings of guilt, asking God for forgiveness
- Psalm 55:1-5, 16-17— feelings of worry and fear
- Psalm 103:1-5, 8-12—feelings of gratitude and thankfulness

Connect the Story
(about 5 minutes)

Select five teenagers to go to the various walls in your meeting space and take down the colored posters (with feelings written on them) and bring them to the front. Hold up the white "Reality" piece of poster board, and explain that it will represent the part of the big story of the Bible that you've explored today. Ask each of the volunteers to tear off a medium-sized piece of his or her colored poster, and invite each one to glue it to the center of the poster. The pieces can overlap in a colorful collage. (They should do this quickly; it should be a rather random collage, not a work of art.)

While these volunteers are working, invite the rest of the group to share their reactions to the psalms that were read. Ask questions like:

- Did you know such extreme emotions were in the Bible? Does it surprise you? Why or why not?

- What stood out to you most from what we just read?

When the volunteers are done, put the poster on the floor to dry, and have them join the rest of the group.

(Keep the poster for Study 12.)

Respond to the Story
(about 15 minutes)

Invite teenagers to write their own psalms, expressing their thoughts, emotions, and questions honestly to God. Suggest they use one of the experiences and feelings from the past week that they identified at the beginning of the session.

Pass out the "Write Your Own Psalm" handout, one per student. Briefly highlight the ideas on the handout for writing psalms, but stress that they can use whatever format they like. Also encourage teenagers to look at the psalms in their Bibles to get more ideas.

Invite everyone to find their own space in the room in which to work. Play some instrumental music in the background to set the tone. Encourage teenagers to just write what's on their heart—they don't have to make it perfect.

When there are three to four minutes left, ask teenagers to find partners. Prompt them to share their psalms with each other if they feel comfortable. If they don't want to read their psalms because their pslams are too personal, that's OK—they can just talk about the experience of writing the psalms.

Wrap up the meeting with a short prayer, and then pass out the "Reality" take-home handouts, one per student. Remind everyone to set aside about 15 minutes (or more) during the week to explore the story more deeply on his or her own using the handout. Explain that they each can tape the handout into a notebook that can serve as an exploration journal throughout the series. They can use their exploration journals as their own personal space for writing down their questions and thoughts.

Key Passage

"My victory and honor come from God alone. He is my refuge, a rock where no enemy can reach me. O my people, trust in him at all times. Pour out your heart to him, for God is our refuge."
- Psalm 62:7-8

This Key Passage can help teenagers grasp the main idea of the study. You can use it in different ways, such as

- writing it on a poster and hanging it up in your meeting space,

- projecting it on a screen,

- inviting teenagers to write it on blank business cards that they can keep in their wallets or pockets,

- prompting teenagers to write it on sticky notes and stick the notes on their mirrors or nightstands at home, or

- challenging teenagers to memorize it on their own during the week.

Aims

This study will help teenagers

- listen to the voice of the prophets calling people back to God.

- understand God's plan: foretelling the coming of the Messiah.

Key Passage

"Now this is what the Lord says to the family of Israel: 'Come back to me and live!'"

- Amos 5:4

Overview

Experience the Story	15 minutes	Teenagers will play a game in which they have to differentiate—and try to obey—competing voices.
Tell the Story	10 minutes	The group will learn that the people of God chose to go their own way even as the prophets called them back to God.
Respond to the Story, Part 1	25 minutes	Teenagers will make speech bubbles and discuss messages that they hear from the culture, family, media, and God.
Connect the Story	5 minutes	You'll create a poster to represent this week's "page" in the big story of the Bible.
Respond to the Story, Part 2	5 minutes	Young people will take a moment to reflect on which message they will listen to in their lives.

Supplies

Make sure you've got

- ❑ Bibles
- ❑ four different types of snacks, such as chips, M&M's, cans of soda, and licorice. You'll want enough snacks so that, at the end of the Experience the Story activity, everyone will have a drink and at least 1 type of snack to eat.
- ❑ 3 adult volunteers
- ❑ plastic bags, paper plates, and napkins (for serving the snacks)
- ❑ your cell phone and an adult volunteer with another cell phone
- ❑ large sheets of card stock or cardboard cut into speech-bubble shapes. You'll need 1 large speech bubble for every 2 or 3 teenagers.
- ❑ old magazines, scissors, glue, markers
- ❑ iPod or CD player for instrumental background music

❏ large piece of white poster board with the following books of the Bible written along the edges like a frame: Hosea, Joel, Amos, Obadiah, Jonah, Micah, Nahum, Habakkuk, Zephaniah, Haggai, Zechariah, and Malachi. (Keep this poster for the final study.)
❏ photocopies of "Communication" take-home handout (p. 157), cut apart, 1 per student

Before the Study

Recruit three other adult helpers to join you in leading the Simon Says activity that opens the study. (If you don't have three adult volunteers, contact three teenagers and ask them to help you lead the opener.) Explain that the group will play Simon Says, but there will be four Simons. You and the three helpers will be the Simons, and you'll stand at the four walls of the room. Let them know that each Simon will have a few snacks of one kind to distribute and he or she will give the snacks to the teenagers who appear to be listening the best. Review how the game will work (see description on p. 87), and ask them to brainstorm various commands ahead of time so the game can move quickly.

Make arrangements ahead of time for one of the other adult volunteers to discreetly call your cell phone one or two times during the beginning of the Tell the Story part of the study. You'll simply ignore the call—acting annoyed at the interruption, but not answering your phone. Be sure your ringer is turned on and, if possible, make it a loud and obnoxious ring tone!

Cut out large speech bubbles (like in comic strips) using card stock or cardboard. You'll need one speech bubble for every pair or trio formed during the Respond to the Story part of the study.

Prepare photocopies of the "Communication" take-home handout (p. 157). Take some time to personally engage with the theme of this study by using the Scripture reflection suggestions below.

ngage

Before the study, set aside some time and space for you to reflect on and engage with the story on a personal level.

A compass points north. It sets a course that you can steer by. It enables you to follow the right path.

But imagine the havoc that a magnet can play with a compass. Bring the magnet close to the compass, and you can tempt the needle off course. You can no longer trust the compass to show you the way. You need to banish the magnet before you can find your path again.

Read Isaiah 1:10-20. The prophets reminded people that there was a true north and that they needed to clear away the distractions and act with integrity. The prophets pointed people back to God and reminded them of the blessings that would follow if they walked in God's ways. Imagine a compass in front of you, pointing the way that you need to go to follow Jesus. What are the "magnets" that swoop in and tempt you from going in Jesus' direction? Name them before God, and recommit yourself to following him. Decide on any action you need to take to banish these magnets from your life.

Pray for your group:
Pray that they would hear God's voice calling them to follow him and that they would understand the blessings that come through walking in God's ways.

THE STUDY

Experience the Story

(about 15 minutes)

Welcome teenagers as they arrive, and then have everyone gather in the center of your meeting area. Stand at one end of the room, and direct your three other volunteer "Simons" to stand at the other three sides of the room, facing the group. Bring three samples of a given snack with you (such as cans of soda), and have each of the other Simons also bring a few snacks with them (a different food per Simon, such as three bags of popcorn or three candy bars.)

Explain to the group that they'll be playing a game of Simon Says, and introduce the other three Simons. Tell the group that you and the other Simons will be issuing commands, such as "Do five jumping jacks," "Hum the 'Star-Spangled Banner,'" "Do your best penguin impression," or "Spin around." Whenever "Simon says" comes before the command, teenagers should do exactly what is said. Whenever "Simon says" doesn't precede the command, they shouldn't follow the command.

Begin by working with the other Simons to very clearly take turns; you issue a command and then the next Simon and then the next Simon. The teenagers will be trying to pay attention to all four givers of instructions. After about two minutes, the commands of the four Simons should begin overlapping so that two of you are talking at any given time. Play this way for one more minute; then shout "Simon says stop!" and have all the other Simons stop issuing commands. Each of the Simons should call out a student by name who he or she thought appeared to do a good job following your instructions. Invite that student to step out of the game, and give him or her the snack. Then each Simon should point out to the group the snack he or she has and say, "If you want this reward, you need to do a better job listening to me!"

Continue playing the game This time with all four Simons talking (or shouting!) commands over one another so that it will be impossible for teenagers to adequately listen to all four of you—they'll need to decide whose commands to focus on. Each

Simon should periodically call out a student's name to give him or her a snack reward.

TIP

If you've got a small group, just have two Simons shouting commands. Do give snacks as rewards, but instead of having those teenagers step out of the game, invite them to keep playing and keep trying to earn more snacks.

Play the game for about seven or eight minutes total; then have everybody take a break and sit on the floor. With the other Simons, bring out the rest of the snacks, and pass them out so that everybody has something to eat and drink. Then discuss the experience, asking the group:

- What was it like to be confronted by so many different voices telling you what to do? How did you feel?

- What strategy did you try? Did you attempt to listen to all four of us? Or did you focus on just one? Why? Which strategy worked better?

- How did you decide who to listen to? Did the reward you hoped you'd get influence your choice? Why or why not?

- Have you ever faced situations in life that have felt a bit like this—like too many voices are trying to tell you what to do? Explain.

Tell the Story
(about 10 minutes)

During this part of the study, the adult volunteer you've made arrangements with ahead of time will call your cell phone once or twice. Have your phone in your pocket or up front with you and set to the side. Whenever the phone rings, say something like, "Oh, I'm sorry, I'm getting a call. Just ignore it." And attempt to keep teaching, despite the ringing sound. Act a bit embarrassed or annoyed, but very obviously do not answer it or turn it off. Just pause a bit in your teaching as it rings, and then continue on.

With everyone gathered together, take about 10 minutes to teach the group the key idea of today's study. Begin by recapping the big story of the Bible so far, emphasizing these key points:

- God created a perfect world that was spoiled by people's disobedience.

- God invited the Israelites back into relationship with him, giving them the promise that if they walked in his ways it would bring life and blessing.

- The people of Israel kept getting it wrong. Their kings did not set a good example, and they kept getting enticed into idolatry by the people around them.

Continue teaching by saying something like: So God sent people to point out where they were going wrong and to encourage them to follow God. These people were called prophets and some of them did some quite dramatic things. Ezekiel, for example, acted out the punishment that was coming to Israel and Judah by laying on his side for 390 days facing a clay model of Jerusalem, eating only bread made from a mixture of grains. He also shaved his head and beard, burned one third of his hair in the city, hid another third with his sword around the city, and scattered the rest to the wind. Sounds slightly crazy, I know, but God was leading him—and he probably got people's attention! Explain to the group that the prophets called people back to follow God. They described the blessings that would follow if people turned back to God. They also talked quite bluntly about terrible things that would happen if the people continued to disobey God. And they dropped big hints about what was to come. They talked about a Messiah or "chosen one" who would come to rule the world justly.

Read Isaiah 9:2, 6-7 and say: *You may have heard these words before. They're pretty famous. They were spoken by a prophet named Isaiah, and they're just one example of things the prophets said about the coming Messiah. Over time, people started to get excited about this Messiah and started hoping for and waiting for him to come.*

Invite a teen volunteer to read aloud Isaiah 1:18-20 while everyone else reads along in his or her own Bible. Explain that it's a typical passage from the books of the prophets because it clearly offers the people a choice: to walk in God's ways and experience blessing or to reject God and to suffer the consequences. They would suffer, not because God had rejected them or would punish them, but because they had chosen to move away from God's protection and wisdom for how best to live life.

Now draw a clear connection to the Simon Says activity, saying something like: *The people had many different voices telling them what to do. Sure, there were the prophets speaking God's Word. But there were also the voices of their culture, enticing them to act certain ways, believe certain things. There were social pressures, political pressures. There were kings and rulers leading the country in totally different directions than what the prophets called for. Though the prophets offered the people God's blessings, the culture enticed them to be selfish, worship idols, act wickedly toward the needy, and live selfish, self-centered lives.*

Hold up your cell phone and say: *God was calling. God was very clearly calling. But they didn't answer God's call. They ignored him—they ignored the words of the prophets.*

Respond to the Story, Part 1
(about 25 minutes)

Invite the group to transition from thinking about the cultural messages in Israel and Judah to the cultural messages today. Ask: *What messages do we hear from the culture and the people around us about what is the best way to live? Which voices in our culture entice us away from God, and which encourage us to follow God?*

Have teenagers form pairs or trios, and give each group a speech bubble, some magazines, scissors, glue, and a marker. Assign each group one of the following areas of life to focus on:

- government
- family/parents

- pop culture/Hollywood
- friends at school
- church
- adults at school: teachers, principal, counselors, coaches
- advertising
- sports/the world of athletics
- media
- grandparents

Explain that you'd like them to think about what that particular voice tells them about how to live. What is the message? What are the enticements or rewards it promises? Or, alternately, what are the punishments it warns of? What does that voice say is the point of life? (There are many different "answers" here—teenagers should focus on their own personal experiences and opinions about each given voice.)

Teenagers should use words, letters, or images from the magazines to create the message from their assigned voice. As needed, they can use their marker to fill in the missing words or images.

Allow groups about ten minutes to create their speech bubbles; then have everyone gather back together. Have someone from each group tell which voice the group was assigned and read the message aloud. Affirm teenagers for their ideas; then have some time for large group discussion. Ask:

- What are some other messages you hear in life that tell you how to live or what to value?

- Which of these voices or messages entice us away from God? How do they do that?

- What are some other examples you've experienced or messages you've heard that try to pull people away from God?

- Why are those voices so powerful? Why do you think so many people follow those types of messages?

- (Refer back to the speech bubbles.) Which of these voices or messages encourage us to live in God's ways?

- What are some other ways you find encouragement to follow God in your life?

TIP

If you have a group of less than twenty teenagers, still have teenagers form pairs or trios, but assign each group two or three cultural voices to discuss and create speech bubbles for. If they don't get them all finished in the allotted time, that's OK—you can bring up those voices during the discussion time and ask the whole group's opinions and ideas.

If you're working with a large group of more than thirty teenagers, assign some of the voices to more than one group.

Connect the Story
(about 5 minutes)

Hold up the poster board with the books of the prophets written on it and say:
Though they often didn't listen, God communicated over and over again to his people through the prophets.

Write the word "Communication" in large letters at the top of the poster, and the word "Prophets" near the bottom. Point out the list of the books of the prophets on the poster, and explain that these are all books of the Bible that contain the words and writings of the prophets as well as stories about their lives.

Then draw a big speech bubble in the middle of the poster. Say something like:
Listen for a moment to something God said to his people through one of the prophets.

Invite a volunteer to read aloud Amos 5:4. In large letters write the words "Come back!" in the speech bubble. Let the group know that this will be the "page" that represents the big story of God you've studied today. Then say something like: God's people heard many voices and many messages calling to them and telling them how to live. So do we. But this simple message God spoke to them through Amos also speaks to us. God says the same thing to people—including us!—today: "Come back to me and live!" Let's consider, for a moment, what else God said through the prophets and how it speaks to us today.

(Keep the poster for Study 12.)

Respond to the Story, Part 2
(about 5 minutes)

Invite young people to find a comfortable space and to lie back and close their eyes. Play some instrumental music to help people relax and focus. Invite them to think about the messages they hear about what makes for a good life. Read aloud the messages that teenagers wrote on the speech bubbles. Then read some of these words from the prophets, pausing after each passage to allow everyone to reflect.

This is what Isaiah said to God's people:

"'Come now, let's settle this,' says the Lord. 'Though your sins are like scarlet, I will make them white as snow. Though they are red like crimson, I will make them white as wool'" (Isaiah 1:18).

This is what God said through Jeremiah:

"'For I know the plans I have for you,' says the Lord. 'They are plans for good and not for disaster, to give you a future and a hope…When you pray, I will listen. If you look for me wholeheartedly, you will find me. I will be found by you,' says the Lord" (Jeremiah 29:11-14a).

This is what Amos had to say:

"Now this is what the Lord says to the family of Israel: 'Come back to me and live!…Do what is good and run from evil so that you may live! Then the Lord God of Heaven's Armies will be your helper, just as you have claimed. Hate evil and love what is good; turn your courts into true halls of justice'" (Amos 5:4, 14-15).

And Zephaniah said this:

"For the Lord your God is living among you. He is a mighty savior. He will take delight in you with gladness. With his love, he will calm all your fears. He will rejoice over you with joyful songs" (Zephaniah 3:17).

You have the same choice as the people of Israel. Will you listen to the voice of God? Will you walk in God's ways? It's up to you.

Allow some quietness at the end of the reflection time, then wrap up the study by praying for your group, asking that they would each hear God's voice calling them to him and that they would follow.

Before everyone leaves, pass out the "Communication" take-home handouts, one per student. Remind everyone to set aside about fifteen minutes (or more) during the week to explore the story more deeply on his or her own using the handout. Explain that they can tape the handout into a notebook that can serve as an exploration journal throughout the series. They can use their exploration journals as their own personal space for writing down their questions and thoughts.

Key Passage

"Now this is what the Lord says to the family of Israel: 'Come back to me and live!'"

- Amos 5:4

This Key Passage can help teenagers grasp the main idea of the study. You can use it in different ways, such as

- writing it on a poster and hanging the poster up in your meeting space,

- projecting it on a screen,

- inviting teenagers to write it on blank business cards that they can keep in their wallets or pockets,

- prompting teenagers to write it on sticky notes and stick the notes on their mirrors or nightstands at home, or

- challenging teenagers to memorize it on their own during the week.

CHALLENGE 8

Aims

This study will help teenagers

- understand that Jesus is God incarnate, came to live among us.

- get a sense of the upside-down nature of the kingdom of God that Christ came to usher in.

Key Passage

"The thief's purpose is to steal and kill and destroy. My purpose is to give them a rich and satisfying life."

- John 10:10

Overview

Experience the Story, Part 1	20 minutes	In small groups, teenagers will make three different kinds of models.
Tell the Story, Part 1	5 minutes	Teenagers will learn that Jesus is God come to earth in human form to finally do what was needed to reverse the effects of the Fall.
Experience the Story, Part 2	15 minutes	Teenagers will make speech bubbles and discuss messages that they hear from the culture, family, media, and God.
Tell the Story, Part 2	3 minutes	The group will learn that Jesus chose common people to be his disciples and carry out his mission.
Respond to the Story/ Connect the Story	17 minutes	Teenagers will consider the parable of the sower and will discuss their own spiritual lives in small groups.

Supplies

Make sure you've got

- ❏ Bibles
- ❏ for Model Station 1: photocopies of the "Model Template" (p. 182) on card stock, markers, tape, scissors
- ❏ for Model Station 2: makeup, hair straightener and/or curling iron, hairspray, dress-up clothes, accessories
- ❏ for Model Station 3: old magazines, scissors, glue, a large sheet of butcher paper or card stock, pens, markers
- ❏ photocopies of the "Model Station Instructions" handout (p. 181), cut apart
- ❏ photocopies of the "Character Cards" handout (p. 183), cut apart. You'll need 1 card per student. (There are 20 cards on the handout, so make additional copies as needed.)
- ❏ iPod or CD player for instrumental background music

- ❑ 1 large piece of white poster board with the word "Challenge" written on it. (Keep this poster for the final study.)
- ❑ sunflower seeds in shells, at least 1 per student
- ❑ bowl
- ❑ white glue
- ❑ marker
- ❑ photocopies of "Challenge" take-home handout (p. 157), cut apart, 1 per student

Before the Study

Jesus' teaching challenged the way people thought and did things. He turned upside down many people's expectations of what the Messiah would be like. So turn some things in your meeting space upside down: books and CDs on shelves, posters, one or two chairs, decorations, and lamps. Don't comment on them—just wait to see if anyone notices.

Prepare three Model Stations in three different areas in your room. For Model Station 1, set out copies of the "Model Template" (p. 182), scissors, markers, and tape.

For Model Station 2, set out a chair, clothing, makeup, and hairstyling supplies.

For Model Station 3, set out card stock, paper, used magazines, glue, scissors, pens, and markers.

Put the appropriate directions from the "Model Station Instructions" handout (p. 181) at each station.

Put all the sunflower seeds in a bowl.

Prepare photocopies of "Character Cards" (p. 183) and "Challenge" (p. 157).

Take some time to personally engage with the theme of this study by using the Scripture reflection suggestions below.

Engage

Before the study, set aside some time and space for you to reflect on and engage with the story on a personal level.

It's difficult to suggest just one passage that sums up who Jesus is and what he came to do! You may want to read some of your favorite stories from the Gospels that show Jesus encountering people and transforming their lives. Or read John 15:1-17 which talks about the relationship that we can have with Jesus: a relationship in which we are loved by him, sustained by him, and a part of his work in this world. Read the passage slowly, savoring each word.

Read it again, letting the truth of Jesus' words sink into your heart and mind.

Now read it one more time, drawing out a word or phrase that you can carry through the day.

Let your experience of this passage lead you into prayer; tell Jesus what is on your heart and mind.

Pray for your group:
Pray that they would have a life-changing encounter with Jesus.

THE
STUDY

Experience the Story, Part 1
(about 20 minutes)

Welcome teenagers as they arrive, and divide them into three even-sized groups. Assign each group one of the Model Stations, and send group members to their station areas to read the instructions and work together to accomplish their given tasks.

Tell teenagers they've got just 15 minutes to accomplish the task at their stations. Here's a quick overview of what they'll be doing:

Model Station 1: Teenagers will make cardboard models of a human being. This involves cutting out a template, coloring it, adding details, and then taping it together.

Model Station 2: Teenagers will create a "fashion model." They will pretend they are doing a fashion shoot for a women's or men's magazine and they will do a makeover on you, one of the other adult leaders, or a member of their group. They'll use makeup, hairstyling supplies, clothing, and accessories to transform their volunteer into a supermodel!

TIP

Depending on the personalities in your group, you may want to purposefully select just girls for Station 2. Or choose guys who are good humored and will have a good time doing a makeover!

Model Station 3: Teenagers will create a list of characteristics of a model or ideal human being. They will create a composite person on a sheet of card stock or butcher paper. The person will be made up of body parts that the group members will cut from magazines. Teenagers will also include written characteristics on the card stock from well-known people.

These station experiences will work best if there are from two to ten people at each station. If you're working with a very small group and have less than six teenagers, eliminate one of the stations. If you've got a larger group with more than thirty teenagers, create six or nine station areas (duplicating the supplies and instructions) so that participants are able to work together at their given tasks.

After 15 minutes, call everyone back together, and invite each Model Station group to show others what it has done.

Tell the Story, Part 1
(about 5 minutes)

Take about five minutes to teach the group, covering the basic idea of today's study. First, tell the group that you're going to explain the next part in the Bible's big story. And then say nothing for about a minute—let there be a short silence. If teenagers try to say anything, just say "shh."

Then remind the group that in the last study they learned about the prophets calling people back to God and the people rebelling and doing their own thing. Explain that after the prophets, there was silence for 400 years. No more prophets, no more words from God.

But there was a growing sense of expectation. People read the Old Testament and believed that God was promising to do something new that would restore their relationship with God once and for all.

Remind everyone that Israel had failed to keep their part in the covenant. They hadn't been the model community that God had invited them to be. The world was still broken. Then explain that God stepped in himself, coming to earth as a human being, Jesus, to finally put things right.

Say something like: *You started this session by making model human beings. We use the word model to mean different things. It can mean a representation in miniature to show what something is like, like a model train. Some of you made this kind of "model" human being using paper.*

Model can also mean a person whose job it is to wear clothes, makeup or accessories for advertising or promotional reasons. We use model this way when we talk about catalogs, runway shows, and magazine covers. Some of you made this kind of model when you did a makeover.

Finally, the word model can mean a standard or example to copy: an ideal. For instance, if you're a model student, you set a good example for the rest of the school. If someone is a model athlete, he or she works hard at training and has great form and expertise. A model athlete is someone others can follow and emulate in sports. This is the kind of model you created by listing attributes of the ideal human being. Explain that the people of Israel were given the opportunity to be God's model community—to show the rest of the world how to live in relationship with God. But as you learned in the past few studies, they failed again and again.

So God sent a new model—his Son, Jesus—to show us how it was meant to be done.

Emphasize these key points to your group:

- Jesus was a model human being because he was the only person who never sinned. He is God's ideal person.

- Jesus is a model human being because he sets an example for us to follow of how to live a life that pleases God.

- But Jesus is also fully divine. He is God in human form.

- When Jesus arrived, he did things differently from what most people expected. Jesus took people by surprise—especially the religious leaders of his day.

Experience the Story, Part 2
(about 15 minutes)

Pass out the Character Cards, one per student, and have everyone stand in a line across one end of the room. Stand at the opposite end of the room, and have everyone face you.

If you have more than 20 people in your group, make extra copies of the cards to pass out. If you have less than 20 teenagers, make sure you pass out a good mixture of "rich" and "poor" characters.

Make sure teenagers have read their Character Cards, and ask them to take on those identities and imagine they describe their lives. Explain that you'll ask participants to take one step forward if their character fits a certain criteria. You won't help them—they each have to decide based on the information on the card whether their character fits the descriptions you call out. Sometimes they'll just have to guess.

When everyone understands the activity, read out these criteria, one by one:

Take a step forward if your character

- has a high school education.
- has a college or graduate school education.
- has a spouse and children or has a strong family around him or her.
- is wealthy.
- is popular.
- is successful in his or her chosen career.
- is in a position of power and influence.
- is likely to have his or her picture in magazines, online, or on TV.

Point out that the rich, successful people are now way out in front of everyone else. Emphasize that these are the types of people that our society applauds and looks up to. This is the model that we are given to aim for.

But then have everyone stay in their spot, but turn 180 degrees so they are facing the other way. Walk to the other end of the room so that you are facing the people who are now out in front. Tell the group that those in the front now are the poor and the powerless.

While they are standing, explain to group members that Jesus encountered, interacted with, and loved the poor and the powerless. He didn't spend much time mingling with the wealthy and the powerful. He spent most of his time hanging out with the lowly—with the nobodies.

Say: S*ome of you may have character cards that are a bit like two people Jesus spent time with: Bartimaeus and Mary Magdalene.*

Bartimaeus was a blind beggar. He sat by the side of the road when he heard Jesus was going past and he cried out "Jesus, Son of David, have mercy on me!"(Mark 10:47). Jesus' disciples tried to shut him up and told him not to bother Jesus. But Jesus called him over and healed him so that he could see.

Mary Magdalene was a demon-possessed woman, but she was healed and became one of Jesus' followers. Church tradition teaches that Mary Magdalene had also been a prostitute. Jesus forgave her, taught her, and valued her when most people rejected her because of her past.

Emphasize for your group that this was the essence of Jesus' teaching: "Those who are last now will be first then, and those who are first now will be last." Explain that the ideas Jesus taught turned the popular ideas of the day upside down. (Point out the upside-down things in your room.) Explain that everyone is invited into God's kingdom; but instead of money and power being a sign of God's blessing, Jesus pointed out that these things can be barriers to having a relationship with God. The people who are now at the front are the types of people who are more likely to know their need for God and to be open to God. The people who are now at the back are the types of people who are more likely to trust in money and power to save them.

Now invite teenagers to form pairs or trios with others standing near them. Have them sit down together and discuss these questions:

- How accurately did the activity we just did represent the way our society values people? What are some examples you can think of that show how our culture values the wealthy and the powerful? How about examples of the way our culture treats the poor and outcasts?

- How do you think the people of Jesus' day reacted to his upside-down approach to what makes people valuable?

- What's your reaction to Jesus' idea that the last will be first and the first will be last? What's appealing to you about this idea? How does it challenge you?

Tell the Story, Part 2
(about 3 minutes)

Teach your group more about Jesus by explaining that Jesus challenged people to turn from living life their way to living life God's way—embracing God's best plan for their lives. Tell the group that Jesus knew that his time on earth would be short, and he wanted to make sure that his work carried on when he was gone. So he chose 12 men to be his disciples. They travelled together, spent time with one another, and Jesus taught them all about the kingdom of God. Jesus healed people, cast evil spirits out of people and taught people about God. And he gave the disciples the opportunity to do the same.

Invite a volunteer to read aloud an example of one of Jesus' teachings in Matthew 10:5-10. Prompt the rest of the group members to read along in their own Bibles. Summarize this passage by saying something like: *Jesus didn't choose well-educated, powerful people to be his disciples; he chose young, ordinary people. Some were fishermen, one was a tax collector. But Jesus gave the disciples an amazing opportunity to learn from him and to grow and he gave them opportunities to put their faith into practice.*

Respond to the Story/Connect the Story

(about 17 minutes)

Hold up the "Challenge" poster and explain that the first four books of the New Testament—Matthew, Mark, Luke, and John—are four unique accounts of Jesus' life and teaching. Tell teenagers the books are called the Gospels, a word which means "good news." As you explain these things, write the word "Gospel" near the bottom of the poster and then, in smaller letters, write Matthew, Mark, Luke, and John. Also write the word "Jesus" in large letters somewhere on the poster as you explain: *The Gospels are all about Jesus. But actually the whole Bible points to Jesus. In a way, everything we've learned in the past few weeks leads directly to Jesus.*

Then set the poster down for now, and pass around the bowl of sunflower seeds. Ask everyone to take one and hold it in his or her hand. Then invite the group to look at another of Jesus' teachings and consider the personal challenge Jesus gives them in the story.

Invite a volunteer to read aloud Matthew 13:3-9 while everyone else follows along in his or her own Bible.

Say something like: *When Jesus told that story, his disciples were a bit confused. Why was he telling stories about sowing seed? Why not just tell people about God? But Jesus knew that stories are a great way of capturing people's interest and getting them to think deeply. He explained that the story was a picture of what God was doing in the world.*

God is like the farmer in the story. His Word, inviting people to be in a relationship with him, is like the seed. God spreads this invitation everywhere, to everyone.

People's hearts are like the different types of ground in the story. Some are like the path—people listen to God but before they can respond, God's invitation is snatched away by those who hate God.

Some people's hearts are like the rocky ground. These people respond to God and they begin to get to know him. But when things get difficult, they give up on God and the relationship dies.

Some people's hearts are like the thorns. These people respond to God's invitation, but worries about life and money crowd in and choke their relationship with God.

Some people's hearts are like the good soil. These people respond to God and begin a relationship with him. And it just gets better and better! They grow strong and healthy. And they produce fruit: Their lives draw other people to God.

Play some instrumental music in the background as you direct teenagers to re-form their pairs or trios from the earlier activity. Invite small group members to take a few minutes to talk about the following questions as they continue to hold the seeds in their hands. Lead this discussion time by asking each question, waiting a few minutes for pairs and trios to talk, and then asking the next question.

- What stands out to you most from this story that Jesus told? How does it speak to you personally?

- Imagine your life as a plant. What things in your life threaten your growth? What may be making the soil of your heart hardened? Or what weeds may be threatening to choke out your faith? What pressures or fears or sins may be trying to steal away your focus on your relationship with God?

- How can the others in your pair or trio pray for you?

While pairs and trios are talking, set the "Challenge" poster on the floor and drizzle white glue all over the middle of it.

When groups have finished praying, invite them each to come up to the poster and stick a seed into the glue. (Allow the poster to dry. Keep it for Study 12.)

Wrap up the meeting with a short prayer, and then pass out the "Challenge" take-home handouts, one per student. Remind everyone to set aside about 15 minutes (or more) during the week to explore the story more deeply on his or her own using the handout. Explain that they each can tape the handout into a notebook that can serve as an exploration journal throughout the series. They can use their exploration journals as their own personal space for writing down their questions and thoughts.

Key Passage

Jesus said: "The thief's purpose is to steal and kill and destroy. My purpose is to give them a rich and satisfying life."

- John 10:10

This Key Passage can help teenagers grasp the main idea of the study. You can use it in different ways, such as

- writing it on a poster and hanging the poster up in your meeting space,

- projecting it on a screen,

- inviting teenagers to write it on blank business cards that they can keep in their wallets or pockets,

- prompting teenagers to write it on sticky notes and stick the notes on their mirrors or nightstands at home, or

- challenging teenagers to memorize it on their own during the week.

Aims

This study will help teenagers

- learn about God's plan of redemption in Jesus and the significance of Jesus' death and resurrection.

- come to appreciate the scope of redemption—all things are made new!

- understand that Jesus wants to redeem us as individuals.

Key Passage

"For God in all his fullness was pleased to live in Christ, and through him God reconciled everything to himself. He made peace with everything in heaven and on earth by means of Christ's blood on the cross."

- Colossians 1:19-20

Overview

Experience the Story	15 minutes	Teenagers will take part in an activity and aim for perfection; every time they make a mistake, they'll have to start over.
Tell the Story/Connect the Story	25 minutes	Teenagers will read about and discuss Jesus' death and learn about the resurrection and how it restored our relationship with God.
Respond to the Story	20 minutes	Teenagers will reflect on the forgiveness that Jesus brings and will have the opportunity to ask for that forgiveness.

Supplies

Make sure you've got
- ❏ Bibles
- ❏ photocopies of the "Failure?" handout (p. 185), one for every 4 teenagers
- ❏ Relationship Cross (p. 169) from Study 3
- ❏ 5 to 15 helium balloons
- ❏ heavy card stock, cut into lengthwise strips; about 4 to 5 strips per student
- ❏ several staplers (if possible, 1 stapler per student)
- ❏ pens
- ❏ scissors
- ❏ 1 large black garbage bag
- ❏ iPod or CD player for ambient background music
- ❏ 1 large piece of poster board with "Solution" written in large letters at the top, the words "Gospels" and "Jesus" written in large letters near the bottom, and a large circle-shaped hole cut out of the center of the poster. (Keep this poster for the final study.)
- ❏ photocopies of the "Solution" take-home handout (p. 158), cut apart, 1 per student

Before the Study

On the day you'll be meeting, get 5 to 15 (or more) biodegradable helium balloons with long strings attached from a florist, grocery store, or party store. Also, cut the card-stock pages into lengthwise strips.

Prepare photocopies of "Failure?" (p. 185) and "Solution" (p. 158).

Take some time to personally engage with the theme of this study by using the Scripture reflection suggestions below.

Engage

Before the study, set aside some time and space for you to reflect on and engage with the story on a personal level.

During this session, you will help your teenagers experience the forgiveness of Jesus—so take some time right now to focus on forgiveness yourself.

Read John 18:1-27 and John 21:1-19.

Peter let Jesus down when he most needed support. But Jesus after his resurrection took the time to reinstate Peter, giving Peter the opportunity to say three times that he loved Jesus. Peter's failure didn't need to be a burden that he carried around with him or something that stopped him from serving Jesus.

Confess your own sins to God. If it helps, write them on pieces of paper and burn or shred them to symbolize God's forgiveness.

John writes, "But if we confess our sins to him, he is faithful and just to forgive us our sins and to cleanse us from all wickedness" (1 John 1:9). Claim this promise for yourself, and thank God for his generous, unlimited, restorative forgiveness.

Pray for your group:
Pray that they realize how Jesus' death and resurrection can transform their lives and this world.

THE STUDY

Experience the Story
(about 15 minutes)

Welcome teenagers as they arrive, and then lead the group in a game of Ha-Ha. In this game, everyone must lay on the floor, with each person placing his or her head next to another person's tummy so that everyone is connected. The first person in the line says "Ha!"; the second person then says "Ha-ha!"; the third person says "Ha-ha-ha!"; and so on. The goal is to get all the way through the entire group without anyone laughing. If anyone does laugh, everybody has to stand up, do five jumping jacks, find a new spot on the floor, lie down, and try again. (If someone starts laughing, it's usually infectious, and everyone else will join in.)

Keep playing (and starting over repeatedly) as the group aims for a perfect round. If they are able to make it through the line once, have them start over, trying to make it through two times in a row without any laughter ensuing.

If you have a small group (ten or less), this game may be too easy—and you don't actually want the participants to be successful. So challenge them to play a tougher game of Ha-Ha by going all the way down the line of players and then going back again (thus doubling the challenge!).

The aim of this experience is for the group to have to start over several times anytime someone messes up (by laughing). Teenagers will probably get more and more frustrated at all the do-overs, and that will make it more and more difficult to complete the task. That's the point!

After the group has tried and failed a number of times, point out that this is a bit like the situation the Israelites were in with regard to sin. They had to offer sacrifices each day for the sins they had committed. And no matter how hard they tried to be perfect, they sinned and had to start all over again offering sacrifices. But Jesus was about to do something that would change that once and for all.

Tell the Story/Connect the Story
(about 25 minutes)

Set the scene by reminding people where you stopped last time in God's big story: Jesus has come as God's promised Messiah and has caused quite a stir with his teachings and miracles. Have teenagers form small groups of four. Give each small group a "Failure?" handout (p. 185), and invite the groups to find a spot in the room where they can follow the instructions and discuss the questions.

After about 10 minutes, have participants stay in their groups and turn their attention toward you.

Say something like: *Thankfully, the story doesn't end here! You just imagined how people felt on the day Jesus died. But two days later, Peter and some of the disciples went to the tomb where Jesus' body had been laid and discovered that the tomb was empty. They saw Jesus—he had come back to life after his death!*

Prompt small groups to read John 20:1-18 aloud together and then discuss the passage. Ask the groups these questions, pausing for few minutes after each one for them to talk:

- Step inside of Peter's mind again. What do you think he thought or felt at this point, after all he'd already felt and seen? Why?

- How about Mary Magdalene? What do you think she felt or thought?

- Imagine for a moment that the story had stopped at Jesus' death—that the part you just read had never happened.

• What difference does this part of the story make? In your opinion, how would history be changed if the story had ended at Jesus' death rather than with his resurrection? Why?

When groups have wrapped up their discussions, have them gather back together and teach your group about the significance of the resurrection by saying something like: *Over a period of 40 days, Jesus appeared to the disciples and many others several times—there was no doubt that he was alive. It's important that we understand what this means. Jesus had conquered death and paid the ultimate sacrifice for sin. Jesus was God's solution to the problem of sin, the way that he was going to restore the world to the state it had been in before the Fall.*

Hold up the battered and twisted Relationship Cross from Study 3. Smooth out the four arms of the cross and explain that Jesus' death and resurrection means that all these relationships can be restored and made new: our relationship with God, our relationships with one another, our relationship with ourselves, and our relationship with the created world. Jesus died to put us right with God and to put right everything that was spoiled and broken in the Fall.

Now hold up the "Solution" poster you prepared ahead of time. Explain that Jesus' death and resurrection was God's solution to the problem of sin and its devastating effects. Tell the group that the large hole in the middle of the poster represents the empty tomb—the symbol of Jesus' resurrection from the dead.

Continue teaching by saying something like: *There are lots of implications of Jesus' death and resurrection that we are going to explore over the next few weeks. But one of the major things that Jesus achieved was doing away with the need to make sacrifices for sins. No longer was there any need for people to offer sacrifices again and again! People didn't have to keep trying to be perfect, keep failing, keep sacrificing, and keep starting over again. Jesus was the ultimate sacrifice—the last sacrifice.*

Now we can experience God's forgiveness by telling God what we have done wrong and asking for him to forgive us. When we do that God responds and welcomes us back with open arms. We will still sin, but every time we do, we can ask for God's forgiveness and receive it.

(Keep the poster for Study 12.)

Respond to the Story

(about 20 minutes)

Invite each person to look for a spot in the room where they can spend some time thinking about the forgiveness that God offers them. As they move around the room, set several piles of card-stock strips around the room, laying pens and staplers by the strips as well. Create a meditative atmosphere by playing some ambient music in the background.

Explain that you're going to read some words to help them privately reflect on what forgiveness means. Tell them that after you read, they can write some things on the paper strips that they want to ask God's forgiveness for, one thing on each strip. After that, they can use the staplers to make those strips into links of a chain. Emphasize that the things they ask forgiveness for will stay private—they should create the links with the writing inside.

When everyone's found a spot and understands the upcoming activity, read the following meditation aloud slowly, pausing often for teenagers to think and reflect in quietness:

Imagine. It's the start of a new day. You get out of bed, have a shower, get dressed, eat some breakfast, set off to explore. The sun is shining. The world feels good, and you're looking forward to the day.

But as you walk, you feel something dragging behind you. There's a weight attached to your ankle. And you know, somehow, that it's there because you yelled at your little brother over breakfast and swore at him. Your anger, the way you treated him, is a weight you need to carry for the rest of the day.

You decide to ignore it, and set off for the mall. You gaze enviously at new iPods in shop windows and wish you could afford one…and the weight on your leg gets bigger. You try to shake it off, but you can't get rid of it. You quietly grab a candy bar from a store as you walk by because you're hungry and you have no money…and the heaviness on your leg grows. You gossip about a guy from school to your friend over the phone…and you can feel that weight weighing you down.

Every time you sin, your burden gets heavier, and it's harder to keep going. What are the things that weigh you down?

And then you see Jesus, a little way ahead of you. He calls your name, and invites you to sit down on a bench next to him. You sit down. It's such a relief not to have to drag the weight any farther.

Jesus looks you in the eye, and asks you about the weight. Why are you carrying all that around with you? Where did it come from? So you tell him everything that's happened today, from breakfast to the gossipy phone call. You're embarrassed talking about some of these things, but it's great to be able to be honest. Jesus listens carefully. Then he bends down and releases the weight from around your ankle. He lifts it, stands up, and says he'll take care of it for you. And off he goes. And you feel clean, and light, and amazingly free.

Spend some time now thinking about what you want to say sorry to Jesus for.

Perhaps things you've said or thought…

Or things you've done…

Or things you should have done but didn't…

You don't need to dig around in your past—Jesus will show you where you need forgiveness. Write each sin down on a strip of card. Take your time. However small, however long ago, however big your sin, Jesus will forgive. Use one strip for each thing you want to confess to Jesus.

When you are ready, use the stapler to make each strip into a link of the chain. Join your chain some others' chains. Then tie the long chain to the string of a balloon, weighing it down.

And pray, asking Jesus to forgive your sin.

Once teenagers start making their chains, get the balloons ready, and help participants start attaching their chains to the helium balloons. The card stock chains should be long enough so they actually weigh down the balloons. (Just to be on the safe side, make sure a teenager is holding on to each balloon's string.)

Once everyone has finished, have the entire group gather around the balloons. (If the weather is good, lead the group outside.)

Read 1 John 1:9 to the group, saying: *In the Bible, God promises that "if we confess our sins to him, he is faithful and just to forgive us our sins and to cleanse us from all wickedness."*

Then walk around, cutting the strings of the balloons so they are free to rise. Allow a moment for everyone to watch the balloons float away. Then collect the chains, and put them in a black garbage bag. Say: *Your sins are forgiven. You are free.*

Lead everyone in a short closing prayer, thanking God for his forgiveness and cleansing.

Wrap up the meeting with a short prayer, and then pass out the "Solution" take-home handouts, one per student. Remind everyone to set aside about 15 minutes (or more) during the week to explore things more deeply on his or her own using the handout. Explain that they each can tape the handout into a notebook that can serve as an exploration journal throughout the series. They can use their exploration journals as their own personal space for writing down their questions and thoughts.

This Key Passage can help teenagers grasp the main idea of the study. You can use it in different ways, such as

- writing it on a poster and hanging the poster up in your meeting space,

- projecting it on a screen,

- inviting teenagers to write it on blank business cards that they can keep in their wallets or pockets,

- prompting teenagers to write it on sticky notes and stick the notes on their mirrors or nightstands at home, or

- challenging teenagers to memorize it on their own during the week.

Aims

This study will help teenagers

- understand the church as the body of Christ and consider their place in it.

- reflect on God's calling to live out their faith in every area of life.

- come to appreciate that they have a responsibility to call others to follow God.

Key Passage

"I will ask the Father, and he will give you another Advocate, who will never leave you. He is the Holy Spirit, who leads into all truth…I will not abandon you as orphans—I will come to you."

- John 14:16-18

Overview

Experience the Story	20 minutes	The group will work together to create a life-size map that represents your community and their lives in it.
Tell the Story	20 minutes	Teenagers will discover what it means to be called to work out our faith in every area of life.
Respond to the Story/ Connect the Story	20 minutes	Young people will make prayer cords with beads.

Supplies

Make sure you've got

- ❏ Bibles
- ❏ paper, pens, crayons
- ❏ several pads of sticky notes
- ❏ tape
- ❏ some random objects from your meeting room or brought from home (see "Before the Study")
- ❏ 7 sheets of butcher paper or flip-chart paper
- ❏ iPod or CD player for worship music
- ❏ photocopies of "Prayer Cord" instructions (p. 187), 1 per student
- ❏ 2-foot leather cord (available at bead stores and craft stores), 1 cord for every student. (You could also use twine, nylon cord, plastic cord, or string.)
- ❏ 7 beads (that fit on the cord) for every student. (Ideally, you'll want seven different colors of beads to represent the seven spheres of life you'll discuss in this study.)
- ❏ extra beads and cord to make one or more sample prayer cords
- ❏ scissors

- ❑ 1 piece of white poster board with these books of the Bible written around the edges like a frame: Acts; Romans; 1 & 2 Corinthians; Galatians; Ephesians; Philippians; Colossians; 1 & 2 Thessalonians; 1 & 2 Timothy; Titus; Philemon; Hebrews; James; 1 & 2 Peter; 1, 2, & 3 John; Jude. (Keep this poster for the final study.)
- ❑ photocopies of "Life" take-home handout (p. 158), cut apart, 1 section per student

Before the Study

Write one of these words or phrases on the top of each of the seven sheets of butcher paper or flip-chart paper: Shopping and Buying; Church; School; Work; Areas of Need; Recreation and Entertainment; Creative Expression.

Clear the floor of your meeting area—putting chairs, furniture, and other objects along the walls of the room—so you've got a large central area.

During the opening activity, teenagers will make a giant "map" of your community on the floor, using objects in the room to represent different landmarks. If the room you're meeting in doesn't have many objects in it (lamps, CD player, trash can, box of tissues, and so on), bring a few random objects, and set them around. For example, bring some books, CDs, a coffee mug, a framed picture, a stapler, a Slinky, and so on.

Prepare the cords and beads for the prayer bracelets. Ideally you'll want some thin leather cord that you can get from a bead shop or craft store, although you can also use yarn, string, nylon cord, or plastic cord. You'll want about seven beads that will thread onto the cord for each person, plus extra beads to make at least one sample cord. Follow the instructions (p. 187) to make one or more sample prayer cords so your group can see what the finished product looks like.

Prepare photocopies of "Prayer Cord" (p. 187) and "Life" (p. 158).

Take some time to personally engage with the theme of this study by using the Scripture reflection suggestions below.

Engage

Before the study, set aside some time and space for you to reflect on and engage with the story on a personal level.

Read Colossians 1:15-20. As you do, keep track of how many times it says "all" or "everything."

Jesus created all things, rules over all things, and will reconcile and restore all things. This world belongs to God, and he wants to see us work out our faith in every part of life, claiming all things for his kingdom.

Think about these areas of life:

> Shopping and Buying
> Church
> School/Work
> Areas of Need
> Recreation and Entertainment
> Creative Expression

Ask God to show you how you can bring each of these areas under his rule in your own life. Pray part of the prayer that Jesus taught us (in Matthew 6:9-13), altering your prayer to address each of these areas. For example, "May your kingdom come…may your will be done as I shop, in my church, in our schools…"

Pray for your group:
Pray that they would have an integrated, holistic view of their life and faith; and pray that they would understand the broad scope of creation and of the coming kingdom. Pray that they would use their gifts to bring in the kingdom of God in every area of life.

Experience the Story

(about 20 minutes)

Welcome teenagers as they arrive, and then challenge them to work together to turn the floor of your meeting space into a giant map of your community. They'll need to follow these instructions:

- Designate which directions represent north, south, east, and west.

- Pick one central "landmark" of your community to put in the middle of room that the rest of the map will be built around.

- Transform objects in your room into buildings and landmarks and place them in the appropriate spots around the room. Participants can label objects with sticky notes or draw pictures and write words on paper and tape the notes or paper to the objects.

When they understand the instructions so far, divide the group into seven smaller subgroups. (Depending on the number of teenagers, you can have them form pairs or subgroups of up to 10 or more.) Tell them that each subgroup will be assigned a category; they'll come up with landmarks that fit the categories for their lives.

Assign groups the following categories:

- Shopping and Buying - any place where they, their friends, or their family members typically buy things or spend money

- Church - various church buildings, locations of meeting places for Christian groups, or any other locations that they think qualify to fit under the label "church"

- School - local high schools, middle schools, nearby universities, or other things they associate with "school"

- Work - locations of where they work, where other teenagers in the youth group work, or where their parents work

- Areas of Need - local spots where there are needy people, organizations that try to help people in need, places where they (or other teenagers) volunteer

- Recreation and Entertainment - any place they like to go for recreation, relaxation, or entertainment; any favorite hangout spots for them and their friends

- Creative Expression - any place that represents creative expression, such as visual arts, movies, music, literature. Encourage them to be creative as they come up with ideas for this one!

Have subgroups start brainstorming and then creating landmarks. Remind them again that they can use any object in the room (within reason!) to be a landmark: a shoe, purse, CD, book, can of soda, and so on. They should put a note on each object that says what it is. (They can decorate it, too, if they want, using paper, crayons, and tape.) They should then decide where the landmark goes on the map of your community in relation to the landmarks that have already been placed there. Clarify that subgroups cannot move landmarks placed by others. Also, it's OK if landmarks are duplicated; they can just be placed next to each other.

Teenagers should keep working to come up with and place landmarks that fit the category they've been assigned. Keep this activity going for about 15 minutes.

TIP

Don't let groups use massive objects (like couches!) as landmarks—they need to select things that will allow room for everyone else's landmarks as well.

TIP

If you've got a smaller sized group (less than 14 teenagers), modify the activity this way. Instead of assigning categories to subgroups, talk through each category one at a time with the entire group. For example, first say "shopping and buying," and have the group work together to come up with a few landmarks and place them. Then go on to "church," and so on. Keep an eye on time, allowing about two minutes for each category.

When time's up, have groups finish and place their final landmarks; then invite group members to tour the "map" they have made, looking around to see the landmarks that other subgroups created. Then have teenagers find seats (in empty places around the floor); ask them to try their best not to move or mess up any of the map landmarks.

Ask the group:

- What do you think of our community map?

- How well does it represent your world—the places that are important in your life?

- Are there any important landmarks in your life that aren't included here? What are they?

- Did you find it easy or hard to come up with important landmarks for your assigned category? Why?

Tell the Story
(about 20 minutes)

Invite the group to recap what they remember about the big story of the Bible as you've covered it so far. Then teach for a few minutes, making sure to focus on Jesus' resurrection. Explain that Jesus appeared to his followers after he rose from the dead. But then he had to go back to be with his Father. Jesus returned to heaven, leaving behind a small band of followers with an important task to do. They were to carry on the work that he had begun: to bring in the kingdom of God. They were to live under God's rule, in ways that pleased God and showed other people the blessings that come from following God. In fact, Jesus said to them that they would do even greater things than he had done! The challenge that Jesus left his followers was to spread the kingdom of God on earth—to create places and communities where God's rules were followed.

Make this link back to Creation: God gave people the world to explore and develop. That's still our task: to apply our faith to every area of life and to serve God in it. We need to consider what God originally intended for each area of life to become like when he created the world, and work to live that out.

Also make this link to the people of Israel: They were supposed to show by their example what it was like to be God's people. Their lives were to show both the blessings and the responsibilities that came with following God.

Say something like: *That's our job, too: to show people around us what God's ways look like in practice—in real, everyday life. Being a follower of Jesus is not just about going to church, although that's an important part of it. It's about being faithful to God in every area of life, including the ones you've represented on the map you've just created.*

Help teenagers form seven new subgroups with people they weren't working with in the opening activity. Give each subgroup a sheet of butcher paper you prepared earlier and some pens, and have subgroup members find a spot in the room where they can sit together.

Say something like: *Take a moment to talk with one another about the area of life written on your paper and consider this question: How should a Christian's life be distinctive in this area? In other words, how should a Christian live this out? How should Christians show their faith in this area of life? How should they be different from the people around them?*

Tell subgroups they have just one minute to talk about and write down their thoughts for their given categories. When a minute has passed, have a "runner" from each subgroup take the butcher paper to the next group (going clockwise around the room). Once subgroups get a new sheet, they have another minute to talk about the new categories, see what others have written, and write down some more ideas.

Keep this going for seven 1-minute rounds. (As needed, allow a little extra time for teenagers to pass the papers to one another.)

> If you've got a small group of teenagers (less than 14), have them form pairs, and give each pair a sheet of butcher paper. Each time a minute has passed, feed the first group a new sheet and collect the sheet from the last group. Not all groups will see all seven sheets, but that's OK.

Once subgroup members have looked at and written on all seven papers, start with one of the categories. Have a subgroup member with that paper read what's written there out loud. Invite comments from the rest of the group, and then share your own thoughts. Also, invite teenagers to share specific examples of ways they've seen other young people live out their faith in that given category. Continue in this pattern for all seven categories. Be sure that these key ideas are covered in your discussion time:

Shopping and Buying: spending our money wisely; following God's values rather than the world's values; making sure that people aren't exploited through what we buy.

Church: being a community that is good news—that worships God, welcomes others, and serves the people around. (This is the place where Christians get equipped and empowered to serve God in all these different areas of life.)

School: applying our faith to our studies and thinking; demonstrating the love of God to our friends.

Work: applying our faith to our workplace; being faithful to God in every area of our work or volunteering; giving our best and serving others.

Areas of Need: reaching out to people in need; caring for the poor and oppressed; sharing the love of God with those in need.

Recreation and Entertainment: enjoying the beautiful world that God has created; making time for rest and play as well as everything else; not participating in overtly sinful forms of entertainment.

Creative Expression: using the gifts God has given us to be creative like him.

Transition from what you've just covered by saying something like: *It sounds like a tall order. How on earth can we do all that? Well, there is one secret ingredient of the story that we haven't talked about so far, but that has been present right from the beginning of the story: God's Spirit.*

Invite a volunteer to read aloud Genesis 1:1 while everyone else reads along in his or her own Bible. Draw teenagers' attention to the truth that God's Spirit was involved at the creation of the world. Then have another volunteer read John 14:15-21 while the rest of you follow along.

Say something like: *People who decide to follow Jesus have God's Spirit living in them. And God's Spirit empowers us to have the right relationships that God intended us to have. It's a big challenge, but the idea is that we work together, trusting God, empowered by the Spirit, supporting one another, building strong relationships that enable us to carry out the mission of God.*

Respond to the Story/Connect the Story
(about 20 minutes)

Invite everyone to make a prayer cord with the cord and beads. Pass out the "Prayer Cord" handouts, and have teenagers follow the instructions on the sheet. Play worship music in the background as teenagers work; keep the atmosphere light, allowing teenagers to talk and relax as they work. As they're making their prayer cords, go around the room and offer help to those who need it.

After 10 or 15 minutes, explain how the prayer cords can be used. Say something like: *Christians have used cords with beads or knots as aids to prayer for centuries. Having something to feel as you pray can give you a rhythm and a focus for prayer.*

Show them how to hold the cord in one hand, take a bead between a thumb and index finger, and say a prayer. Then show how they can move on to the next bead, and so on through the cord. Explain that they can use the cord to pray about the seven areas of life they focused on today. Encourage them to use the cords as guides in their prayer time this week and in the coming months, asking God to show them how they can be faithful to him in each of those areas of their lives.

Hold up the poster you prepared, and explain that it will represent the "page" in the story you learned about in this session. Point to the word "Acts" on the poster, and explain that the book of Acts is like "Part 2" of Luke's Gospel. Acts is the sequel that describes what happened among Christians after Jesus returned to heaven. Then explain that all the other books of the Bible listed on the poster are letters that Christian leaders wrote to groups of Christians to encourage them as they strove to live for God. Write the word "Letters" in bold letters near the bottom of the poster. Then say something like: *The key here is that our faith is not just about church or youth group. It's about every single aspect of our lives. It's about all of who we are.*

Write the word "Life" in large letters at the center of the poster, and then invite a volunteer to tape the sample prayer cord to the poster.

Say something like: *Jesus once taught his disciples how to pray. His prayer is often called the Lord's Prayer or the Our Father. In it, Jesus taught his followers to pray, "May your Kingdom come…May your will be done" (Matthew 6:10).*

Invite the group to pray responsively with you, repeating the words "May your kingdom come and may your will be done" after each phrase you say, as follows:

> Leader: *God, when it comes to how I shop and what I buy…*
> All: **May your kingdom come and may your will be done.**
> Leader: *In our church…*
> All: **May your kingdom come and may your will be done.**
> Leader: *In my school…*
> All: **May your kingdom come and may your will be done.**
> Leader: *In my work now and in the career I will have some day…*
> All: **May your kingdom come and may your will be done.**
> Leader: *In how I respond to people in need…*
> All: **May your kingdom come and may your will be done.**

Leader: *In my relaxation and in my fun…*
All: **May your kingdom come and may your will be done.**
Leader: *In my music, art, writing, and other forms of creative expression…*
All: **May your kingdom come and may your will be done. Amen.**

Pass out the "Life" take-home handouts, one per student. Remind everyone to set aside about 15 minutes (or more) during the week to explore the story more deeply on his or her own using the handout. Explain that they each can tape the handout into a notebook that can serve as an exploration journal throughout the series. They can use their exploration journals as their own personal space for writing down their questions and thoughts.

(Keep the poster for Study 12.)

Key Passage

"I will ask the Father, and he will give you another Advocate, who will never leave you. He is the Holy Spirit, who leads into all truth….I will not abandon you as orphans—I will come to you."
- John 14:16-18

This Key Passage can help teenagers grasp the main idea of the study. You can use it in different ways, such as

- writing it on a poster and hanging the poster up in your meeting space,

- projecting it on a screen,

- inviting teenagers to write it on blank business cards that they can keep in their wallets or pockets,

- prompting teenagers to write it on sticky notes and stick the notes on their mirrors or nightstands at home, or

- challenging teenagers to memorize it on their own during the week.

11

Aims

This study will help teenagers

- understand that Jesus will return at some point in the future.

- realize that the scope of Christ's redemption is as wide as the scope of Creation and the scope of the Fall.

- discover their role as they wait for Jesus' return.

Key Passage

"Then I saw a new heaven and a new earth…I heard a loud shout from the throne, saying, 'Look, God's home is now among his people! He will live with them, and they will be his people. God himself will be with them. He will wipe every tear from their eyes, and there will be no more death or sorrow or crying or pain. All these things are gone forever.'"

- Revelation 21:1a, 3-4

Overview

Experience the Story	10 minutes	Teenagers will watch a movie clip and discuss how the future is often portrayed in the media.
Tell the Story	20 minutes	The group will discuss Jesus' return and what it means.
Respond to the Story/ Connect the Story	30 minutes	Teenagers will create a city of peace by turning junk into art; then they will create a final page for the big story and pray about their hopes and dreams.

Supplies

Make sure you've got

- ❏ Bibles
- ❏ The Day After Tomorrow DVD or similar film (see suggestions on p. 139)
- ❏ TV and DVD player
- ❏ student art pieces saved from Study 3
- ❏ newspapers and magazines
- ❏ materials for junk modeling: cardboard boxes, duct tape, masking tape, aluminum foil, scissors, glue, twine, metal clothes hangers, other random pieces of junk
- ❏ basic art supplies like markers, tempera paints, glitter-glue pens, construction paper, and so on
- ❏ 1 large piece of white poster board. (Keep this poster for the final study.)
- ❏ photocopies of "Hope" take-home handout (p. 159), cut apart, 1 per student

Before the Study

In this session, you'll get young people thinking about the vision of the future that they get through films. Most films about the future are bleak, showing society disintegrating or disaster overcoming us. This outline suggests showing a clip from The Day After Tomorrow because of the current concern about climate change—it taps nicely into our deep fears about what we are doing to our planet! But feel free to select your own movie clip from a recent film about the future, such as I Am Legend; I, Robot; Minority Report; Gattaca; Deep Impact; or Independence Day.

If you're using The Day After Tomorrow, cue the DVD to about 0:45:29, right after three men get on a bus and one says "I love buses; this is so much fun." The clip you'll show lasts until about 0:49:04, with an image of water surrounding the library.

Gather together the student art pieces from Study 3 that depict brokenness. Set the art along one wall of your meeting room. (If you've got time, hang the art on the wall in a nice display.)

Also, save copies of the newspaper throughout the week, as well as a few recent news magazines. Take just a few minutes to tear out pages that contain "bad news" about current events: tragedies, war, crime, political fights, corruption, environmental degradation, divorce, teen pregnancies, vandalism, gang violence, terrorism, and so on. You'll want three to five news stories for every pair or trio of teenagers.

Collect a bunch of cardboard boxes and other random pieces of junk. If you can, get people from your church family to collect boxes and other junk and donate it to your group for this study. Set all of the junk supplies and art supplies against the wall that is opposite the student art from Study 3.

Prepare photocopies of "Hope" (p. 159).

Take some time to personally engage with the theme of this study by using the Scripture reflection suggestions below.

Engage

Before the study, set aside some time and space for you to reflect on and engage with the story on a personal level.

Read Revelation 21:1-4. This is the promise of the future that we can look forward to.

What are your dreams for the renewed heavens and earth? What do you long to see healed and restored? Write down one dream

- for yourself.
- for your family and friends.
- for the young people you work with.
- for your church.
- for your community.
- for your country.
- for the world.

Bring these dreams to God, and cry out to him for healing in these areas. Ask for wisdom to know what to look for and work toward now, and what needs to wait until Jesus returns.

Pray for your group:
Pray that they would catch a glimpse of God's power and desire to bring about change in our world and that they'd get a sense of how they can be involved in the work of God's kingdom.

Experience the Story

(about 10 minutes)

Welcome teenagers as they arrive, and then ready the group to watch a clip from The Day After Tomorrow. First explain the background: *Sam Hall is in New York taking part in a school quiz competition with his friends Laura and Brian. The world is in the middle of a dramatic climate change, but no one realizes how serious it is except Sam's dad, who is a climatologist. Sam, Laura, and Brian are trying to get home in the middle of a major storm.* Play the clip, starting at about 0:45:29, after three men get on a bus and one says, "I love buses; this is so much fun." Stop the clip at about 0:49:04, with the image of water surrounding the library.

After the clip, ask the group:

- What's your response to this clip? What thoughts or feelings does it evoke in you?

- What are some other movies about the future you've seen over the years? How do they portray the future?

  (Help them brainstorm here if needed. You could bring up movies like I Am Legend; I, Robot; Minority Report; Gattaca; Deep Impact; or Independence Day.)

- Why do you think most movies or TV shows about the future depict it as very bleak?

- Do you think the future will be like that? Why or why not?

Tell the Story
(about 20 minutes)

Say something like: *Imagine you've got a friend who is very skeptical of Christianity. You've had lots of conversations with your friend about the Bible and what it's all about. So your friend flat out asks you this: "If Jesus' death and resurrection restored everything that was ruined by the Fall, why is there still so much brokenness and suffering and evil in the world?" How would you answer? What do you think?*

Prompt teenagers to turn to partners. Allow pairs at least three minutes to wrestle with these really tough questions and attempt to develop adequate answers. Then invite volunteers to share their thoughts with the rest of the group.

Direct pairs to read in Matthew 13:24-30 one of Jesus' stories. Ask them to talk about the story together and try to put its meaning into their own words.

If necessary, remind them of the discussion about the parable of the sower from Study 8 (in Matthew 13:3-9), and prompt them to recall what the seed and the ground represented in that story.

Have everyone gather back together, and invite volunteers to share their interpretation of Jesus' parable in Matthew 13:24-30. Then take a few minutes to teach the group more about what Jesus' teaching here means. Say something like: *In Study 3 we heard about Satan who tempted the first people to reject God's ways. Satan has been active in the world, spreading evil ever since and there has been no shortage of people joining in. Satan even tried to tempt Jesus to do wrong. And so we can see the wheat and the weeds in our own world: the beauty of God's world and his invitation to have a relationship with him alongside the brokenness of sin.*

Present this idea to your teenagers: Jesus' kingdom is both "now" and "not yet." Tell them that Jesus came to bring in the kingdom of God. We can experience some parts of that kingdom now, but we need to wait for the rest. Now we can have a new relationship with God because of Jesus' death and resurrection. But Jesus is coming back some day, and that's when the whole of creation will be renewed. The Bible says there will be a new heaven and a new earth—the ultimate in recycling!

Ask the group:

- What words or images come to mind when you hear the word heaven?

- How is heaven often portrayed in pop culture?

Say: *Let's look at what the Bible says about heaven.*

Invite a volunteer to read Revelation 21:1-4 aloud while everyone else reads along in his or her own Bible. Say something like: *When Jesus returns, all the brokenness in the world will be dealt with once and for all. We live in a world where the weeds are growing alongside the signs of God's kingdom. But there will come a time for the harvest, when everything will be pulled up and the weeds will be destroyed.*

We don't know exactly what the new heaven and new earth will be like, but we do know that

- *we will be able to live with God and talk with him face to face like the first people who lived on earth.*

- *it will be a place of wholeness, where there is no longer any brokenness, pain, crying or death.*

- *just like Jesus had a body when he was resurrected, so we will have resurrection bodies.*

- *it will be our home, a place for us to live with God for all eternity.*

Explain that not everyone wants to be part of this future. God offers us a choice, just like he offered the Israelites a choice. If we choose to live in relationship with God, we can be part of this future. If we choose to ignore God, we will spend eternity separated from him. The Bible calls this hell.

Tell the group that the Bible describes this future reality using images and metaphors to help us understand it and many of these can be found in the book of Revelation. The story of the Bible starts in a garden (the Garden of Eden) and ends in a city (the new City of Jerusalem).

Explain that the task God gives his people is to work to bring the kingdom of God into every area of life. And it is also to hunger and thirst for the future new creation, where we will live with God and where all sin and brokenness will be destroyed once and for all. Because it is creation renewed, the future we look forward to is a rich and full one! Heaven isn't about wearing white nightgowns and playing harps while sitting on clouds!

Respond to the Story/Connect the Story
(about 30 minutes)

Set out a few piles of the "bad news" newspaper and magazine pages throughout the room. Direct teenagers to form pairs or trios. Ask small-group members to grab a few pages from one of the piles and take the pages to an area of the room where the group can sit. Prompt them to take a moment to scan through the news stories they have. Then ask groups:

- • What are some other examples of bad news you've read or heard about in our world or in our community in the past few weeks?

Read Revelation 21:22-27 aloud so everyone can hear. Invite teenagers to think about what God's city will be like in the new creation. It will be a city of peace, of plenty, of wholeness.

Draw their attention to their art pieces from Study 3 that depict brokenness in the world. Say something like: *It's not hard to find examples of brokenness and sin in our world. Brokenness surrounds us. It's constantly in the news. It touches every aspect of our lives. But God's city won't be touched by it. It will be completely different.*

Challenge teenagers to respond to the images and stories of brokenness by creating an element of God's city that can represent brokenness restored. To do so, they'll use pieces of junk and art supplies and transform them into sculpture or models of some type.

Share these ideas to help them start brainstorming:

- In response to the issue of homelessness, a pair might use a cardboard box to create a house with an open door. It can represent a place that's always open to people in need.

- In response to the issue of violent crime, a trio might create a model "recycling factory" where guns can be turned into useful tools rather than used to kill or hurt others.

- In response to the issue of physical disability and disease, a group might make a sculpture out of wire, newspaper, and duct tape that looks like crutches tossed to the ground. It can represent the fact that crutches will no longer be needed because everyone will be healed.

Point out all the pieces of junk and art supplies teenagers can use, and also encourage them to use the newspaper and magazine articles if they'd like. Also, if they want, they can incorporate their own pieces of art from Study 3 into their new sculptures. Encourage them to use their imaginations! You're not saying they have to make things that will literally be in the new creation—just symbols or sculptures that point to what type of place it will be.

Aim to allow at least 20 minutes for pairs and trios to work on their junk sculptures. (Be sure to give a five-minute warning when time is almost up!) Encourage teenagers to talk, ask questions, and have fun as they work. If groups get done early, invite them to wander around and look at what others are making.

While teenagers are working on their sculptures, grab a few "bad news" stories, as well, and use scissors to cut out big block letters that spell the word "HOPE." (Or, if some participants finish their junk sculptures early, ask them to help you do this.)

When teenagers have finished their creations (or when time's up), invite them to bring their junk sculptures up to the front. Ask someone from each small group to briefly explain what they made.

Congratulate participants on their creativity and on the important truths they represented in their sculptures.

Then hold up the blank white poster board and say: *Over the past 11 weeks, we've learned all about the Bible's big story. Today we've talked about the main point of the very last book of the Bible.*

Write the word "Revelation" near the bottom of the poster. Explain that the book of Revelation is also a letter, like those they learned about last week. Tell them it was written by the Apostle John. But Revelation is more than just a letter—it contains details of the amazing vision of the future that God allowed John to see.

Then have four volunteers tape the letters that spell "HOPE" in the middle of the poster. Say: *We live in a broken world, but Revelation tells us of a hope that shines through the darkness. Jesus will come again. Jesus' kingdom will come in fullness. There will be a new heaven—a city of God. And if we have a relationship with Jesus, we will live there with him. That's real hope.*

Tell the group that in your next meeting you'll put all the parts of the big story together and you'll have time to talk about any questions they might have about what you've discussed so far. Then lead everyone in a short closing prayer, thanking God for his forgiveness and cleansing.

Pass out the "Hope" take-home handouts, one per student. Remind everyone to set aside about 15 minutes (or more) during the week to explore things more deeply on his or her own using the handout. Explain that they each can tape the handout into a notebook that can serve as an exploration journal throughout the series. They can use their exploration journals as their own personal space for writing down their questions and thoughts.

(Keep the poster for Study 12.)

Key Passage

"Then I saw a new heaven and a new earth…I heard a loud shout from the throne, saying, 'Look, God's home is now among his people! He will live with them, and they will be his people. God himself will be with them. He will wipe every tear from their eyes, and there will be no more death or sorrow or crying or pain. All these things are gone forever.'"

- Revelation 21:1a, 3-4

This Key Passage can help teenagers grasp the main idea of the study. You can use it in different ways, such as

- writing it on a poster and hanging the poster up in your meeting space,

- projecting it on a screen,

- inviting teenagers to write it on blank business cards that they can keep in their wallets or pockets,

- prompting teenagers to write it on sticky notes and stick the notes on their mirrors or nightstands at home, or

- challenging teenagers to memorize it on their own during the week.

CONTINUING THE STORY

12

Aims

This study will help teenagers

- celebrate the end of the study series together.

- review what they've learned throughout the series.

- learn about ways they can dig deeper into the Bible.

Overview

Celebrate the Story	10 minutes	Teenagers will hang out, eat snacks, and have fun together.
Connect the Story	20 minutes	The group will recap the key points of the entire study series.
Respond to the Story	30 minutes	Teenagers will share with one another how they've been personally impacted by the study and will learn about ways to study the Bible more on their own.

Supplies

Make sure you've got

- ❑ Bibles
- ❑ all 11 "pages" of the big story—the poster board pieces you and your teenagers created during each Connect the Story segment
- ❑ optional: tape
- ❑ lots of celebratory food and drinks, pizza, soda, and ice cream
- ❑ iPod or CD player for upbeat music as well as some instrumental background music
- ❑ samples of other Bible study materials teenagers could use in the future
- ❑ optional: new Bibles to give to teenagers as a way to mark their journey through God's Word
- ❑ paper and pens

Before the Study

Get lots of great food and drinks set up for a fun, laid-back celebration together. Set out (or hang up) the 11 pages from the Connect the Story segment of each study session. (Be sure they're in the right order!)

Also gather some Bible study materials you can show teenagers to give them ideas about how they can grow deeper in their own personal study of God's Word.

Ask the leaders of your church if they'd be willing to purchase new Bibles for all of the teenagers. You can give them during this final celebration time together.

TIP LIVE is a New Living Translation of the Bible designed specifically for teenagers and young adults that includes life-changing devotional material. Go to group.com/live/ for more info.

Engage

Before the study, set aside some time and space for you to reflect on and engage with the story on a personal level.

You made it! Well done! Congratulations on leading this study series and on providing a stimulating, loving environment in which young people can encounter the God of the Bible.

Read Ephesians 3:14-21. Pray this whole prayer for yourself. Then pray this prayer for the teenagers in your group, trusting that God will continue to work in their hearts and lives and enable them to live fully for him.

THE STUDY

Celebrate the Story
(about 10 minutes)

Welcome everyone as they arrive and invite them to enjoy some food and drinks together. Play upbeat music in the background as everyone hangs out together, talks, and has a good time.

Connect the Story
(about 20 minutes)

Draw everyone's attention to the 11 pages from Connect the Story that are now around the room. Take about one to two minutes per page, simply inviting teenagers to share what they remember as the key ideas of each study session. If teenagers have brought their journals, invite them to flip through the pages to spark their memories.

Do your best to draw out the key points from them rather than reteaching everything at this point. Affirm teenagers for their input. Keep things lighthearted and open during this part, encouraging teenagers to get up to get more food as they want.

Respond to the Story
(about 30 minutes)

Have everyone sit in a circle, and do a few discussion "rounds" together. What you'll do is ask a question, and then each person in the circle will have a turn to respond to the question.

TIP If you've got a large group, form several circles of 8 to 10 teenagers each. Have an adult leader join each group to lead the discussion.

Using the rounds format, ask teenagers:

- Has your view of the Bible changed by doing this study series? If so, how?

- What have you learned about the Bible during these past 12 weeks?

- What was the highlight of the studies for you? Why?

- What questions do you still have about the Bible?

Take a few minutes to tell your group members about some ways they can dig deeper into the Bible on their own. Pass out some sample Bible study materials, and share about what you'll be studying next in your youth group. Present the idea of each teenager pairing up with a friend to encourage each other in their exploration of Scripture. Also, invite the teenagers themselves to share any ideas they have of things that could help them grow in their engagement with God's Word.

If you have new Bibles to give to the teenagers, do so now. Encourage them to really dive in and make that copy of the Bible their own. If the Bible has devotional materials or study notes, point them out and explain how they can be used.

Wrap up by inviting teenagers to spread out around the room and write letters to God about what they've gotten out of the study and what their hopes for the future are. Play instrumental music in the background as teenagers write. Encourage your group members to respond to God by deciding to play their part in God's living story.

Appendix

Permission to photocopy all handouts in the Appendix section from
Through the Bible granted for local church use.

1 Story

What was this week all about?

The Bible is not just a random collection of ancient old books. It has a story running through it from the beginning to the end. It's a story about God's action in this world. And although the Bible has an end, God's story doesn't. It's still going on because God is still involved in this world. What's more, you're invited to be part of this story, to live for God today.

Key Passage

Read these words from the Bible, and think about what they mean:

"All Scripture is inspired by God and is useful to teach us what is true and to make us realize what is wrong in our lives. It corrects us when we are wrong and teaches us to do what is right. God uses it to prepare and equip his people to do every good work."

– 2 Timothy 3:16-17

Reflect

What's your opinion about the Bible? Write it in your journal and don't hold anything back. This is for you and you only, so don't worry about offending anyone.

Do

Interview a friend (via text, e-mail, or IM) by asking a simple question: What do you think about the Bible? Why?

Accept whatever your friend says—don't argue or try to persuade. Just think about his or her opinion and how it compares and contrasts with your own.

Connect

Flip to the back of your journal, and designate 12 blank pages to be your Connect the Story section. Each week you'll use a page to draw your own symbol that represents what you've learned about the Bible. This week was the beginning of the story—you haven't really dived in yet. So use the first blank Connect page to draw a picture frame. Doodle the frame anyway you'd like but keep the inside empty to represent your openness to learning more about God's big story.

Old Testament

Genesis
Exodus
Leviticus
Numbers
Deuteronomy
Joshua
Judges
Ruth
1 Samuel
2 Samuel
1 Kings
2 Kings
1 Chronicles
2 Chronicles
Ezra
Nehemiah
Esther
Job
Psalms
Proverbs
Ecclesiastes
Song of Songs
Isaiah
Jeremiah
Lamentations
Ezekiel
Daniel
Hosea
Joel
Amos
Obadiah
Jonah
Micah
Nahum
Habakkuk
Zephaniah
Haggai
Zechariah
Malachi

New Testament

Matthew
Mark
Luke
John
Acts
Romans
1 Corinthians
2 Corinthians
Galatians
Ephesians
Philippians
Colossians
1 Thessalonians
2 Thessalonians
1 Timothy
2 Timothy
Titus
Philemon
Hebrews
James
1 Peter
2 Peter
1 John
2 John
3 John
Jude
Revelation

2 Source

What was this week all about?

God created an amazing world for us to live in. Look around at the detail and complexity of the world, and it will show you something of what God is like. God has given us the ability to be creative, too, and he wants us to develop and explore the world he has given us. We need to look after the world in a way that shows what God is like. God created us to have good relationships—with God, with ourselves, with other people, and with creation.

Key Passage

Read these words from the Bible, and think about what they mean:

"Then God looked over all he had made, and he saw that it was very good! And evening passed and morning came, marking the sixth day. So the creation of the heavens and the earth and everything in them was completed."

– Genesis 1:31–2:1

Reflect

What are your favorite parts of the world God made? Think big (like stars and planets) and small (like insects or molecules). Brainstorm at least twenty things God created that you really like, and list them in your journal.

Do

Try and find some space outside to look at the beauty of God's creation. If you live in the city, go for a walk in the park or watch the sunrise or sunset from your yard. If you live in a more rural area, find a field to walk in. Savor what you see, breathe deeply, and thank God for the world he has created.

Connect

Flip to the Connect the Story section in the back of your journal. Imagine it is your job to create a logo that represents the idea of God creating the world. What colors, shapes, letters, or words would you use? On the second page of the Connect section, draw your first draft of a possible logo that represents this part of God's big story.

Old Testament

Genesis
Exodus
Leviticus
Numbers
Deuteronomy
Joshua
Judges
Ruth
1 Samuel
2 Samuel
1 Kings
2 Kings
1 Chronicles
2 Chronicles
Ezra
Nehemiah
Esther
Job
Psalms
Proverbs
Ecclesiastes
Song of Songs
Isaiah
Jeremiah
Lamentations
Ezekiel
Daniel
Hosea
Joel
Amos
Obadiah
Jonah
Micah
Nahum
Habakkuk
Zephaniah
Haggai
Zechariah
Malachi

New Testament

Matthew
Mark
Luke
John
Acts
Romans
1 Corinthians
2 Corinthians
Galatians
Ephesians
Philippians
Colossians
1 Thessalonians
2 Thessalonians
1 Timothy
2 Timothy
Titus
Philemon
Hebrews
James
1 Peter
2 Peter
1 John
2 John
3 John
Jude
Revelation

4 Invitation

What was this week all about?

God couldn't just leave his beautiful creation broken and ruined by sin. He wanted to put things right. So he chose a man called Abram and said that all of Abram's descendants would be God's chosen people. God gave his chosen people, Israel, laws to show them how to live. They were meant to be a living example of the good relationships that God intended people to have. They were given huge privileges, but they also had to play their part. God blessed them so that they could be a blessing to other people.

Key Passage

Read these words from the Bible, and think about what they mean:

"The Lord had said to Abram, "I will make you into a great nation. I will bless you and make you famous, and you will be a blessing to others. I will bless those who bless you and curse those who treat you with contempt. All the families on earth will be blessed through you."

- Genesis 12:1-3

Reflect

God's laws, summarized in the Ten Commandments (Exodus 20:1-17) can guide people in how to rightly obey God...but can also be tough to live out. What parts of God's laws do you find most difficult to consistently put into practice? Write your thoughts in your journal.

Do

Think about how you can be a blessing to other people. Decide to do surprise acts of kindness this week for your friends and family, and even for people you don't get along with!

Connect

Flip to the fourth page of the Connect the Story section you've created in your journal. Write the word "Invitation" in big letters at the top. Then write two more words. First, think about the privilege of having a unique relationship with God that God offered to the people of Israel, and write any word you want to that describes that invitation. (For example, you could write "special" or "close" or "chosen.")

Next, think about the responsibility God gave his people: believing in God and following his laws. Write any word you want to that describes that responsibility. (For example, you could write "hard," "rules," or "perfect.")

---

3 Broken

What was this week all about?

God created a perfect world, but it's far from perfect now! Satan tempted Adam and Eve to disobey God. When they did, it affected the whole of creation and all of us throughout time. Because, be honest, wouldn't you have done exactly the same thing? Our relationship with God was ruined, and so were our relationships with others, with ourselves, and with the rest of creation. We live in a broken world that is spoiled by sin.

Key Passage

Read these words from the Bible, and think about what they mean:

"We are made right with God by placing our faith in Jesus Christ. And this is true for everyone who believes, no matter who we are. For everyone has sinned; we all fall short of God's glorious standard. Yet God, with undeserved kindness, declares that we are righteous. He did this through Christ Jesus when he freed us from the penalty for our sins."

- Romans 3:22-24

Reflect

Think about your experience of sin and brokenness and how it has affected:

- your relationship with God.
- your relationships with others.
- your relationship—with yourself.
- your relationship with creation.

List one effect you've personally experienced or sin you've participated in for each of these categories. Remember—your journal is private, so be as brutally honest with yourself as you can.

Do

Think about what you can do to put right just one of the relationships that we thought about this week. For example, you could

- spend time talking to God, asking God to help you know him better.
- spend time with a friend or a member of your family, having fun together and building your friendship.
- do something to take care of yourself, like exercising or taking a nap.
- take a step to care for God's creation, like walking instead of going in the car, recycling, turning off lights you don't need on.

Connect

Flip to page 3 in the Connect the Story section in the back of your journal. Write the word "Broken" at the top or along the side of the page. Then tear away part of the page, and throw it out to represent the damage sin has done to creation.

Old Testament

Genesis
Exodus
Leviticus
Numbers
Deuteronomy
Joshua
Judges
Ruth
1 Samuel
2 Samuel
1 Kings
2 Kings
1 Chronicles
2 Chronicles
Ezra
Nehemiah
Esther
Job
Psalms
Proverbs
Ecclesiastes
Song of Songs
Isaiah
Jeremiah
Lamentations
Ezekiel
Daniel
Hosea
Joel
Amos
Obadiah
Jonah
Micah
Nahum
Habakkuk
Zephaniah
Haggai
Zechariah
Malachi

New Testament

Matthew
Mark
Luke
John
Acts
Romans
1 Corinthians
2 Corinthians
Galatians
Ephesians
Philippians
Colossians
1 Thessalonians
2 Thessalonians
1 Timothy
2 Timothy
Titus
Philemon
Hebrews
James
1 Peter
2 Peter
1 John
2 John
3 John
Jude
Revelation

5 Choice

What was this week all about?

Inside all human beings is the instinct to worship something. That means to have something in your life that becomes your goal, that you devote time and energy to, and that you make sacrifices for. We were designed to worship God, but if we don't, then we end up worshipping something else. The Israelites were tempted by the pagan religions around them and worshipped statues made of silver and gold. We are more likely to worship money, fame, success, and power. We each have a choice to make—who or what will we worship?

Key Passage

Read these words from the Bible, and think about what they mean:

"You must not have any other god but me. You must not make for yourself an idol of any kind or an image of anything in the heavens or on the earth or in the sea. You must not bow down to them or worship them, for I, the Lord your God, am a jealous God who will not tolerate your affection for any other gods."

- Exodus 20:3-5a

Reflect

Fill a page in your journal with at least 15 examples of idols that people worship today.

Do

Throughout history, people have bowed or knelt before kings and rulers as a way to show honor and submission. Find time to be alone and pray to God. When you pray, kneel down and bow your head. Let your posture represent your commitment to have God at the center of your worship, not modern idols.

Connect

Flip to the fifth page in the Connect the Story section of your journal. Write the word "Choice" at the top. Then, along one side of the page, write the word "God." On the other side of the page, write or draw something that represents a modern idol that tempts you. Draw a line down the middle of the page, between the word "God" and the idol, to represent the reality that we each have to choose who or what we will worship.

Old Testament

Genesis
Exodus
Leviticus
Numbers
Deuteronomy
Joshua
Judges
Ruth
1 Samuel
2 Samuel
1 Kings
2 Kings
1 Chronicles
2 Chronicles
Ezra
Nehemiah
Esther
Job
Psalms
Proverbs
Ecclesiastes
Song of Songs
Isaiah
Jeremiah
Lamentations
Ezekiel
Daniel
Hosea
Joel
Amos
Obadiah
Jonah
Micah
Nahum
Habakkuk
Zephaniah
Haggai
Zechariah
Malachi

New Testament

Matthew
Mark
Luke
John
Acts
Romans
1 Corinthians
2 Corinthians
Galatians
Ephesians
Philippians
Colossians
1 Thessalonians
2 Thessalonians
1 Timothy
2 Timothy
Titus
Philemon
Hebrews
James
1 Peter
2 Peter
1 John
2 John
3 John
Jude
Revelation

6 Reality

What was this week all about?

Although the Bible was written thousands of years ago, it's all about people and how they relate to God. And although our lives are very different from the way people lived during the time the Bible was written, we share a lot of the same worries, joys, fears, and frustrations. The Bible is "God-breathed"—inspired by God who is the creator of life and who knows how life is meant to work. So it's not surprising that we'll find help in the Bible for any problem in life we are trying to deal with. Some books in the Bible are called wisdom books because they give us insights into life and the nature of reality. But we can find wisdom for how to live throughout the entire Bible.

Key Passage

Read these words from the Bible, and think about what they mean:

"My victory and honor come from God alone. He is my refuge, a rock where no enemy can reach me. O my people, trust in him at all times. Pour out your heart to him, for God is our refuge."

- Psalm 62:7-8

Reflect

Sometimes people get the impression that we always have to be positive, hopeful, upbeat, and formal when we talk with God. Do you think that's true? Why or why not? Jot down some notes that explain your point of view.

Do

Set aside half an hour when you won't be disturbed. Sit down with God, and tell God exactly how you feel about life, about yourself, about him. You may want to express your feelings in different ways—through writing, singing, making music, creating art, or writing a poem. Be creative and be real.

Connect

Flip to the sixth page in the Connect the Story section at the end of your journal. Doodle four faces on the page: a happy face, a sad face, a mad face, and a scared face. Then write "Reality" on the page to show that we can be real with God about our experiences and feelings.

Old Testament

Genesis
Exodus
Leviticus
Numbers
Deuteronomy
Joshua
Judges
Ruth
1 Samuel
2 Samuel
1 Kings
2 Kings
1 Chronicles
2 Chronicles
Ezra
Nehemiah
Esther
Job
Psalms
Proverbs
Ecclesiastes
Song of Songs
Isaiah
Jeremiah
Lamentations
Ezekiel
Daniel
Hosea
Joel
Amos
Obadiah
Jonah
Micah
Nahum
Habakkuk
Zephaniah
Haggai
Zechariah
Malachi

New Testament

Matthew
Mark
Luke
John
Acts
Romans
1 Corinthians
2 Corinthians
Galatians
Ephesians
Philippians
Colossians
1 Thessalonians
2 Thessalonians
1 Timothy
2 Timothy
Titus
Philemon
Hebrews
James
1 Peter
2 Peter
1 John
2 John
3 John
Jude
Revelation

❽ Challenge

What was this week all about?

God gave his people chance after chance to come back to him, but they refused. So God decided to get more personally involved. God sent his Son, Jesus, to earth as a model human being to show us how to live and how to find our way back to God. Jesus was completely human, but also fully divine—he was God in human flesh. And when Jesus came, he took people by surprise. He turned upside-down people's understanding of what was important in life. And he chose twelve disciples who could carry on his work after him.

Key Passage

Read these words from the Bible, and think about what they mean:

Jesus said: "The thief's purpose is to steal and kill and destroy. My purpose is to give them a rich and satisfying life."

– John 10:10

Reflect

This session you discovered what the Bible is all about: Jesus. There are lots of opinions out there about Jesus. What do you think about him? Who was he? Who is he? Write a few sentences that sum up what you think of Jesus based on what you know so far.

Do

Now consider this question: How will you respond to Jesus? That's the biggest decision of your life. Maybe you've already decided to follow Jesus; maybe you've got lots of questions; maybe you're not sure what all the fuss is about. This week take some steps on your journey toward Jesus. Think, pray, talk to your leader or your friends about it.

Connect

Flip to the eighth page in the Connect the Story section at the end of your journal, and write the word "Challenge" at the top to represent the challenge Jesus gives us to know him and to live rightly.

Remember the story Jesus told about seeds? (You can look it up in your own Bible—it's found in Matthew 13:3-9.) Think for a moment about what kind of ground your heart is, and then draw a picture on the page of yourself as a plant. Has the seed taken root? Are you growing strong? Are you being choked by weeds? Are you a small plant in need of water and nourishment? You're your plant however you'd like.

Old Testament

Genesis
Exodus
Leviticus
Numbers
Deuteronomy
Joshua
Judges
Ruth
1 Samuel
2 Samuel
1 Kings
2 Kings
1 Chronicles
2 Chronicles
Ezra
Nehemiah
Esther
Job
Psalms
Proverbs
Ecclesiastes
Song of Songs
Isaiah
Jeremiah
Lamentations
Ezekiel
Daniel
Hosea
Joel
Amos
Obadiah
Jonah
Micah
Nahum
Habakkuk
Zephaniah
Haggai
Zechariah
Malachi

New Testament

Matthew
Mark
Luke
John
Acts
Romans
1 Corinthians
2 Corinthians
Galatians
Ephesians
Philippians
Colossians
1 Thessalonians
2 Thessalonians
1 Timothy
2 Timothy
Titus
Philemon
Hebrews
James
1 Peter
2 Peter
1 John
2 John
3 John
Jude
Revelation

❼ Communications

What was this week all about?

God saw that his chosen people, the Israelites, were worshipping false idols instead of God. So he sent people called prophets to speak to the Israelites on his behalf. The prophets pointed out where the people were going wrong. They reminded them of the blessings that came with walking in God's ways, and the consequences that would follow if they kept on rejecting God. The prophets often used dramatic ways of getting their message across. They also talked about the future, giving clues to God's plan to send a messiah to save his people.

Key Passage

Read these words from the Bible, and think about what they mean:

"Now this is what the Lord says to the family of Israel: 'Come back to me and live!'"

– Amos 5:4

Reflect

There are many voices and many messages competing for your attention. Some of them are calling you away from God, enticing you to live by other values or to value the wrong things. Take a moment to think about one specific voice that is drawing you away from God and the way of life God calls you to—such as a friend, a TV show, a song, a social group—or perhaps a certain message from movies or advertising that you've started to believe. You may be listening (and believing) without even realizing it! Write down the voice and its message and then in just a sentence or two about how you think it contradicts what God may be calling you to.

Do

You could be a prophet telling people that God loves them! Send a text message to a friend with a truth about God, or leave a Bible verse on a sticky note where someone will find it.

Connect

Flip to the seventh page in the Connect the Story section at the end of your journal, and draw a quick picture of a cell phone to represent God's "call" to you. Think about your response. Will you listen? Will you answer?

10 Life

What was this week all about?

Jesus returned to be with God, his Father, and he left the disciples behind to carry out his work. The challenge that Jesus left his followers, which can include us if we choose to get involved, was to spread the kingdom of God on earth, to create places and communities where God's rule was followed. He wants us to have the healthy relationships with God, with ourselves, with creation and with others that God intended for us. Sounds like a lot of work? Well, Jesus has left his Spirit with us to help us to carry that out. God's Spirit will live within us if we invite him, to equip us and empower us to be like Jesus.

Key Passage

Read these words from the Bible, and think about what they mean:

"I will ask the Father, and he will give you another Advocate, who will never leave you. He is the Holy Spirit, who leads into all truth…I will not abandon you as orphans—I will come to you."

– John 14:16-18

Reflect

God's Spirit is with you, ready to help you live for God. If you have a faith relationship with Jesus, God's Spirit is literally in you! Think about the difference between trying to live for God on your own strength versus relying on God's Spirit to help you. Jot down a few sentences that describe that difference.

Do

Use your prayer cord to pray that God's kingdom will come in these areas of your life:

- Shopping and Buying
- Work
- Recreation & Entrtainment
- Church
- Areas of Need
- Creative Expression
- School
- Recreation

Connect

Flip to the tenth page in the Connect the Story section of your journal. Jesus calls you to have a faith that touches every aspect of your life. Is that how you normally view faith? Draw a circle, and pretend it's a pie chart that represents your life. Write the word "LIFE" beneath it.

Now think about how much of your life you currently let your faith into—is it 2 percent? 25 percent? 50 percent? Blacken in a segment of the "pie" to show how much of your life is infused with faith. Then blacken in the rest of the pie to represent what it looks like to have your whole life devoted to Jesus.

---

9 Solution

What was this week all about?

To his followers, Jesus' death seemed like a complete disaster. They couldn't understand how things could have gone so wrong. But their despair turned to joy when they realized that Jesus had come back to life! He had beaten death. He had conquered sin. Jesus did away with the need for sacrifices for sin to be made over and over again. Now we can come to God at any time, ask for his forgiveness, and receive it. Jesus has restored our relationship with God and also our relationships to ourselves, to others, and to the world we live in.

Key Passage

Read these words from the Bible, and think about what they mean:

"For God in all his fullness was pleased to live in Christ, and through him God reconciled everything to himself. He made peace with everything in heaven and on earth by means of Christ's blood on the cross."

– Colossians 1:19-20

Reflect

How does it feel to be forgiven? Write a few words that capture what forgiveness feels like.

Do

Decide that you will talk to God regularly, bringing him your successes, your hopes, your dreams, your disappointments, and your failures. Know that God loves you and forgives you. And if you find that hard to believe, talk to your youth leader about it. Sometimes that really helps.

Connect

Flip to the ninth page in the Connect the Story section of your journal. Write the word "Solution" at the top of the page, and then use large, unique letters to write the word "Jesus" on the page. Use block letters; bubble letters; graffiti-like letters; or letters with swirls, zigzags, or stripes. Make Jesus' name your own instant work of art.

11 Hope

What was this week all about?

If Jesus came to put right everything that has been ruined by sin, why is there so much pain and brokenness in the world? Well, we can experience some of God's kingdom now, but we need to wait for the rest. Now we can have our relationship with God restored. But we will have to wait until Jesus returns before we see the whole of creation made new. When Jesus does come back, there will be a new heaven and a new earth where we can walk with God face to face. Sin and Satan will finally be destroyed once and for all.

And you have a choice about whether you are part of that future. If you choose to live in relationship with God, you can look forward to an eternity in the new heaven and new earth. If you choose to ignore God, you will spend eternity separated from God. It's up to you.

Key Passage

Read these words from the Bible, and think about what they mean:

"Then I saw a new heaven and a new earth…I heard a loud shout from the throne, saying, 'Look, God's home is now among his people! He will live with them, and they will be his people. God himself will be with them. He will wipe every tear from their eyes, and there will be no more death or sorrow or crying or pain. All these things are gone forever.'"

- Revelation 21:1a, 3-4

Reflect

God wants to make everything new, to put right everything that is spoiled and broken in this world. Write down your hopes and dreams

- for yourself.
- for your community.
- for your family and friends.
- for the world.

Do

Talk to God about the dreams you wrote down. Ask God what his dreams are for these people and places. Ask God how you can get involved in his work in the world. Then move beyond just thinking and praying. Take a step—do something to put your hope into action. Invite a friend to join you as you take a small step to make a difference in the world.

Connect

Flip to the eleventh page in the Connect the Story section of your journal. Write the word "Hope" at the top of the page, and then sketch a city skyline to represent the coming new City of God. (Make your skyline as elaborate or as simple as you'd like.)

How Does It End?

The Characters

Chrissie: Likes to be a leader, quite bossy, never admits mistakes, expects to give orders and for others to follow them. Doesn't like to be challenged.

Nick: The joker of the group—always goofing around and trying to make people laugh. Good at cheering people up. Likes to be liked.

Samantha: Good organizer, quietly gets on with what needs to be done. Caring—very aware of what other people are thinking and feeling. Doesn't like being taken for granted.

Phil: A worrier. Good at thinking through detail but then worries about it all. Quite pessimistic and expects things to turn out badly, but is very loyal to his friends.

Don't worry if you haven't got two boys and two girls in your group. Just change the names and genders of as many characters as you need to. For example Chrissie can become Christopher, Nick can become Nicki, Samantha can become Sam, and Phil can become Philippa!

The Story So Far…

Act 1

These four friends are organizing a fundraising event for a cancer charity at a cool restaurant downtown they've rented out, and it's going to be awesome. Their band is going to be headlining, some of their friends are organizing a fashion show, one of the seniors from their school is going to do some stand-up comedy, and there are a couple of other bands playing, too. A deejay will then finish off the evening. Phil's mom has just recovered from cancer which is why they've chosen that charity. They're really excited about it. They've put a lot of effort into organizing it, and it's all going really well.

Act 2

Disaster! They were just finishing a band practice when all four cell phones rang nearly at the same time, each with bad news. The restaurant was accidentally double-booked for the night of their event and the other group that reserved it has priority because they booked first. The deejay has had all his equipment stolen from his car, including his CD collection. The people organizing the fashion show haven't been able to get any clothes despite visiting all the shops in town. And Samantha's friend told her that Chrissie has been bragging that she can get Sam to do whatever she tells her to. Chrissie and Samantha have a massive fight and end up not talking to each other. It's all gone horribly wrong.

Act 3

The four friends have a meeting to try and sort it out. Nick has some suggestions for a new venue, but keeps cracking jokes and getting on people's nerves. Phil suggests they could just skip the fashion show part, but he's worried that then the event won't be as good. They've heard that the deejay will be able to get money from his insurance for all his stolen equipment and CDs, but they're not sure if there's enough time for him to get new stuff. But Chrissie and Samantha are still not speaking, and Samantha is just sitting in the corner doing her nails. They're trying to put things right, but it's just not working.

Act 4

Phil gets them to go and talk to a teacher at school about it the next day. The teacher manages to get them to sit down and talk about what happened. He makes Chrissie and Samantha listen to each other's point of view, when before they'd just been shouting at each other. He offers the school hall as a venue, plus all the sound and light equipment they need. And his cousin is a fashion student and might have some contacts for the fashion show. But there are only two days to go. And they've been arguing so much they haven't rehearsed as a band for ages.

But What Happens Next?

It's up to you to create Act 5, the ending of the story. You need to be true to the first four acts and to the characters. Of course, characters can change in a story, but there has to be a reason for it.

Think about your selected character for a couple of minutes. What do you think he or she would do next? Then talk with the others in your group. You have 10 minutes to create an ending. Get ready to show it to everyone else!

Characters

Photocopy and cut these strips apart. You'll want to have about three or four strips per student.

- -

Eve
The first woman in the Bible. She gave in to temptation and disobeyed God.

- -

Noah
Was mocked by others for obeying God and building an ark. His ark rescued his family and some animals from a great flood.

- -

Abraham
He was an old man when God promised him a son.
He was called a "friend" of God.

- -

Moses
Doubted his ability to make a difference in the world. But with God's power on his side, he led the people of Israel out of slavery in Egypt towards the Promised Land.

- -

Deborah
A strong woman leader of Israel who took her people into battle. Others relied on her for inspiration, confidence, and courage.

- -

David
A king of Israel who was a great warrior and a talented poet. He also messed up in a huge way by committing adultery and orchestrating a murder—but God forgave him.

- -

Hannah

A woman who was mistreated by family members and heartbroken because of infertility. She cried out to God for a son and then gave her child back to God.

Elijah

A bold, gutsy prophet who challenged Baal worshippers to a contest to see who the real God was.

Esther

A beautiful queen who made a tough choice in the face of tremendous pressure. Her choice ended up saving her people from death.

Daniel

Taken to a foreign country as a young man, he stayed true to God despite the pressure of the pagan culture around him.

John

A wild man who told people that Jesus was coming. John spoke truth to power so boldly that he was jailed and eventually executed for making enemies of powerful people.

Jesus

The Son of God who became a human and lived on earth.

Peter

A common fisherman who followed Jesus but who often said wrong things.

Paul

A man who vehemently hated Christians, until he met Jesus and became one.

Mary Magdalene

A woman with a dark past who discovered God's forgiveness.

Priscilla

A leader in the church that began after Jesus rose from the dead.

Lydia

A businesswoman who became a Christian. A church met in her home.

Timothy

A young Christian who was called to be a leader. Despite his age, he led a church and changed lives.

Judas

One of Jesus' disciples who couldn't understand some of Jesus' teachings. Judas eventually betrayed Jesus.

Lazarus

A friend of Jesus who died. Jesus brought him back to life.

Who Made…

1. Who wrote this?

Hence! home, you idle creatures get you home:
Is this a holiday? What! Know you not,
being mechanical, you ought not walk
upon a labouring day without the sign
of your profession? Speak, what trade art thou?

2. Who created the characters Charlie Brown, Snoopy, and Woodstock?

3. Who first said these famous words?

I have a dream that my four little children will one day live in a nation where they will not be judged by the color of their skin but by the content of their character.

I have a dream today.

4. Which company first brought the classic video game characters Mario (and his brother, Luigi) and Zelda to life through home video game systems?

5. What did Mark Zuckerberg create and launch when he was just 19 years old? (Circle your answer.)

    A. A five-star gourmet restaurant
    B. A homemade rocket that actually crashed into the moon
    C. Facebook
    D. His own film production company:
       Z-berg Pictures

6. Who wrote this?

Harry was bleeding. Clutching his right hand in his left and swearing under his breath, he shouldered open his bedroom door. There was a crunch of breaking china: he had trodden on a cup of cold tea that had been sitting on the floor outside his bedroom door...

...He looked around; the landing of number four, Privet Drive, was deserted.

7. Think back to your U.S. History class. Who's the author behind the Declaration of Independence?

8. This man has created over 100 cartoon characters including Apu, Smithers, Nelson Muntz, and Santa's Little Helper. Who is he?

Who Made…
Quiz Answers

Check your answers against these, and then rip up your answers and throw them in the trash so others can't see what you've written.

1. William Shakespeare (This is the beginning of his play Julius Caesar.)

2. Charles M. Schultz

3. Rev. Martin Luther King Jr.

4. Nintendo

5. C. Facebook

6. J.K. Rowling, in Harry Potter and the Deathly Hallows

7. Thomas Jefferson

8. Matt Groening, the creator of The Simpsons

Relationship Cross

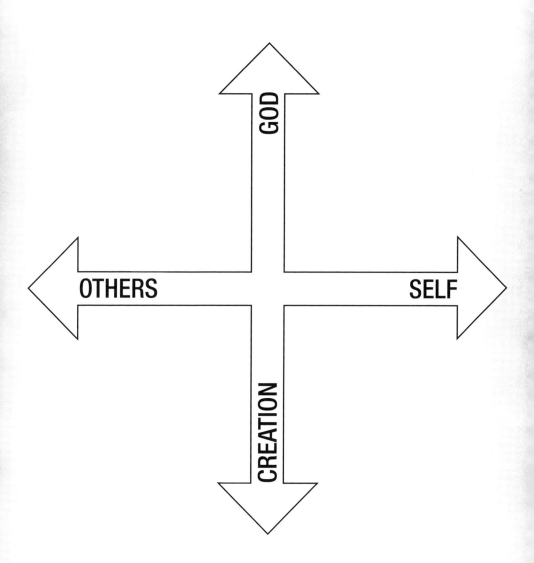

Top Critics

You need to work together to present a movie review to everyone else. So first things first: Choose a movie that you all enjoyed or that you all hated. (It doesn't need to be a recent movie.) Don't spend too long choosing! (If you can't think of a movie, select a TV show, music album, or video game to critique.)

Your review should tell the story of the film, without any plot spoilers. You need to tell people what you liked about the film and highlight what you felt didn't work. Your presentation doesn't need to be long—just one or two minutes.

But remember: Throughout this activity, one of you has to stay blindfolded, one of you has to wear earplugs, one of you can speak only in a foreign language (pick one you've studied in school!), and one of you can only communicate through writing—no talking!

All of you have to take part in the presentation to the rest of the group. Be as creative as you like!

The Ten Commandments

1 God spoke all these words: I am God, your God, who brought you out of the land of Egypt, out of a life of slavery. No other gods, only me.

2 No carved gods of any size, shape, or form of anything whatever.

3 No using the name of God in curses or silly banter; God won't put up with the irreverent use of his name.

4 Observe the Sabbath day, to keep it holy. Don't do any work.

5 Honor your father and mother so that you'll live a long time in the land that God, your God, is giving you.

6 No murder.

7 No adultery.

8 No stealing.

9 No lies about your neighbor.

10 No lusting after your neighbor's house—or wife/husband or servant or maid or ox or donkey. Don't set your heart on anything that is your neighbor's.

(Summarized from Exodus 20:1-17 in The Message paraphrase of the Bible.)

The Kings (and Queens) of the Bible

Jeroboam: evil, gave the people two golden calves to worship (Israel)

Rehoboam: evil, constantly at war with his brother (Judah)

Abijah: evil, as bad as his father (Judah)

Asa: good, got rid of idol worship (Judah)

Nadab: evil, killed by the man who took over as king (Israel)

Baasha: evil, just like Jeroboam (Israel)

Elah: evil, killed by Zimri who succeeded him (Israel)

Zimri: evil, set the palace on fire around him (Israel)

Omri: evil, worse than all the other kings (Israel)

Ahab: very evil, worshipped Baal (Israel)

Jehoshaphat: good, like his father Asa (Judah)

Ahaziah: evil, Ahab's son (Israel)

Joram: evil, another of Ahab's sons (Israel)

Jehoram: evil, married Ahab's daughter (Judah)

Ahaziah: evil, only reigned for one year (Judah)

Jehu: good, wiped out all of Ahab's descendants (Israel)

Athaliah: evil, Ahaziah's mother who ruled as queen, tried to destroy the royal family (Judah)

Joash: good, started his reign when he was seven years old (Judah)

Jehoahaz: evil, Jehu's son (Israel)

Jehoash: evil, waged war against Judah (Israel)

Amaziah: good, killed the officials who had killed his father (Judah)

Jeroboam II: evil, caused the people of Israel to really suffer (Israel)

Azariah (also known as Uzziah): good, became king at 16, had leprosy (Judah)

Zechariah: evil, assassinated after six months (Israel)

Shallum: evil, assassinated the previous king, only reigned for one month, was assassinated (Israel)

Menahem: evil, took heavy taxes from the people (Israel)

Pekahiah: evil, ended up assassinated (Israel)

Pekah: evil, assassinated (Israel)

Jotham: good, rebuilt some of the temple (Judah)

Ahaz: evil, became king at age 20, sacrificed his own son in fire (Judah)

Hoshea: evil, Israel taken into exile so he was the last king (Israel)

Hezekiah: good, destroyed idols, trusted God (Judah)

Manasseh: evil, became king at age 12, set up idols (Judah)

Amon: evil, worshipped idols, ignored God, assassinated (Judah)

Josiah: good, became king at age 8, found God's law again (Judah)

Jehoahaz: evil, carried off to Egypt by Pharaoh Neco (Judah)

Jehoiakim: evil, land invaded by Babylon but he rebelled (Judah)

Jehoiachin: evil, reigned for three months, taken prisoner (Judah)

Zedekiah: evil, conquered by Babylon, last king of Judah (Judah)

Idols Today

Use these questions to talk about the issue of idolatry in your small group.

- Why do you think the kings and people of Israel worshipped idols? What might have motivated them?

- Though we don't worship god-shaped idols in our culture today, what similarities might exist between Israel's worship of idols and our culture?

- Do you think people today treat the following things as idols? If so, share some examples from everyday life or popular culture:

  - money, wealth, possessions
  - sports
  - the way we look, being thin or fit
  - work/career
  - celebrity, being famous
  - power

- None of these things are bad in and of themselves. So what turns something that's "neutral" into an idol?

- What about your own life? What may be some idols in your life—without you even realizing it?

Shades of Emotions

Happy

amused	high	thrilled
blessed	jolly	upbeat
blissful	joyful	
cheerful	jubilant	
chirpy	light	
content	merry	
delighted	overjoyed	
ecstatic	playful	
elated	pleasant	
excited	pleased	
glad	satisfied	
gleeful	sunny	

Sad

bitter	forlorn	upset
blue	gloomy	weeping
dejected	glum	wistful
depressed	grieving	
despairing	heavy-hearted	
despondent	hurting	
discouraged	low	
dismal	mournful	
distressed	pensive	
down	pessimistic	
downcast	sorry	

Angry

annoyed	infuriated
bad tempered	irate
bothered	irritated
displeased	livid
enraged	outraged
exasperated	raging
frustrated	resentful
fuming	sulky
furious	tense
incensed	ticked off
indignant	uptight

Scared

afraid	panic-stricken
aghast	petrified
alarmed	shaken
anxious	shocked
apprehensive	startled
daunted	stressed
fearful	tense
frightened	terrified
horrified	timid
intimidated	worried
nervous	
on edge	

Feeling Left Out

I need advice. I'm feeling a bit down. I was in a group of friends, and we used to go out to someone's house or to the movies almost every weekend. After a while it seemed like we hadn't gotten together for a while. But it occurred to me that they hadn't stopped getting together—they'd just stopped inviting me. They invited some other people who basically replaced me in the group. They're all still very friendly to me when I talk to them, but they still keep getting together without inviting me. I thought of inviting them over to my house, but my house is boring and there's not a lot to do. Any ideas?

What advice would you give to this person?

Helpful Hints

"Putting confidence in an unreliable person in times of trouble is like chewing with a broken tooth or walking on a lame foot" (Proverbs 25:19).

"A friend is always loyal, and a brother is born to help in time of need" (Proverbs 17:17).

- -

A Big Flirt

I need advice. My best friend has been going out with his girlfriend for six months. She's really nice, but my friend is always flirting with other girls whenever she's not around. He says it's harmless and that's just what guys do. I think he's not being fair to his girlfriend, who I really like. I think he should act like he does when she's around even when she's not. We've had a few arguments about it. What do you think about his behavior, and what should I do?

What advice would you give to this person?

Helpful Hint

"Can a man scoop a flame into his lap and not have his clothes catch on fire? Can he walk on hot coals and not blister his feet? So it is with the man who sleeps with another man's wife. He who embraces her will not go unpunished" (Proverbs 6:27-29).

Losing Too Much Weight

I need advice. My friend is really obsessed with her weight, and I'm worried that she's endangering her health. She's pretty skinny already, but she wants to be thinner. We have this routine when we're in each other's rooms—we stand in front of the mirror and stick out our stomachs to make ourselves look fat. We then chant at each other, "Fat slob! Fat slob! Lose some weight!" It started out as a joke and probably sounds really stupid, but I think she's taking it seriously now. She's always asking me whether she needs to lose more weight. I think she's going too far. What should I do? I don't want her to stop being my friend.

What advice would you give to this person?

Helpful Hints

"An honest answer is like a warm hug"(Proverbs 24:26, The Message).

"Some people make cutting remarks, but the words of the wise bring healing"
(Proverbs 12:18).

Drinking Too Much

I need advice. Every time I go out with my friends I always drink a lot. They say I make them laugh and get me to drink more. I love the feeling that drinking gives me, but a few times I've gotten really sick because I got too drunk. Sometimes I can't even remember what happened. I'm not sure if I have a problem. Isn't this just normal? I do feel depressed sometimes, but that's not why I drink. Do you think I need help?

What advice would you give to this person?

Helpful Hints

"Wine produces mockers; alcohol leads to brawls. Those led astray by drink cannot be wise"
(Proverbs 20:1).

"Who has anguish? Who has sorrow? Who is always fighting? Who is always complaining? Who has unnecessary bruises? Who has bloodshot eyes? It is the one who spends long hours in the taverns, trying out new drinks. Don't gaze at the wine, seeing how red it is, how it sparkles in the cup, how smoothly it goes down. For in the end it bites like a poisonous snake; it stings like a viper" (Proverbs 23:29-32).

Write Your Own Psalm

There are tons of ways to write psalms. You can write whatever you like—it just needs to be honest and real. So choose the subject of your psalm first. Is there anything you really want to talk to God about? What do you want to write about?

If you aren't sure where to start, here are some ideas you might find helpful.

An Acrostic Psalm

Some of the psalms in the Bible are acrostics—each line of the psalm starts with a different letter of the Hebrew alphabet. Why not try writing one? You could use our alphabet, or choose a word that's the theme of your psalm. Here are two examples:

After school I went

Bowling with my friends

Caitlynn and

Dan.

Each moment was so

Full of friendship and laughter.

Good friends are

Hard to find, and

I

Just want to thank you, God, for friends

Like these.

May we always look out for one another and

Never take one another for granted.

Depression:

Each day is such an effort.

People don't understand how

Real my feelings are. Will I

Ever be able to laugh again?

Save me, God, from this despair.

Send me friends who will understand me.

I don't want to suffer like this

Or to feel so low. God, come

Near to me and help me.

A Psalm With a Refrain

Psalm 136 starts:
"Give thanks to the Lord, for he is good!
His faithful love endures forever.
Give thanks to the God of gods.
His faithful love endures forever."

Every other line of the psalm is exactly the same: "His faithful love endures forever."

If there's a strong message you want to get across in your psalm, you could use that message as a refrain, repeating it over and over, like Psalm 136. In the other lines, you could tell a story or write whatever you want.

Rewrite a Psalm

One of the best-known psalms is Psalm 23: "The Lord is my shepherd."
But not many of us know any shepherds these days, so the psalm loses
some of its meaning. Think of a similar role that's around today: someone who cares for others, protects them, and provides for them. And
then rewrite the psalm using images and ideas that fit that role. For
example, you could start, "The Lord is my teacher…"

Look up Psalm 23, and follow the structure of the psalm. You could copy
the beginning of some of the lines and then add on your own ideas.

Add to a Psalm

Use one of the psalms that you heard during the study that fits the
theme you want to explore. Add your own verses to it every so often.
You'll end up with a chunk of the psalm and then your own words; then
another chunk of the psalm, and so on.

- Psalm 13—feeling helpless and sad

- Psalm 23—feeling safe and secure in God's hands

- Psalm 37:3-5—feelings of delight and trust

- Psalm 51:1-10—feelings of guilt and asking God for forgiveness

- Psalm 55:1-5, 16-17—feelings of worry and fear

- Psalm 103:1-5, 8-12—feelings of gratitude and thankfulness

Model Station Instructions

Model Station 1

Make a model human being.

Cut around the outline of the person. Use markers to add details and to color the person's hair and clothes. Then fold the model, stick the tabs in, and tape everything together.

- -

Model Station 2

Make a model human being.

This is your chance to do a makeover! Select someone in your group (or grab one of the adult leaders), and have him or her be the model. Have the model sit in the chair while the rest of you use the supplies at this station area to turn your volunteer into a model fit for a magazine photo shoot. You won't have much time, so you need to be quick and creative!

- -

Model Station 3

Make a model human being.

What does an ideal human being look like? What kind of person are they? What characteristics do they have?

On the large sheet of paper, work together to create a picture of a model human being by cutting different body parts from celebrities, models, and athletes out of magazine pictures. For example, you could use the legs of Kobe Bryant for fitness and speed. Be creative! Also, write or draw other characteristics all around the edge of the paper, such as the humor of Will Ferrell, the self-discipline of Tiger Woods, the brains of your physics teacher, or the compassion of your mom. Who are the people who inspire you? Add their qualities around the edge of the paper.

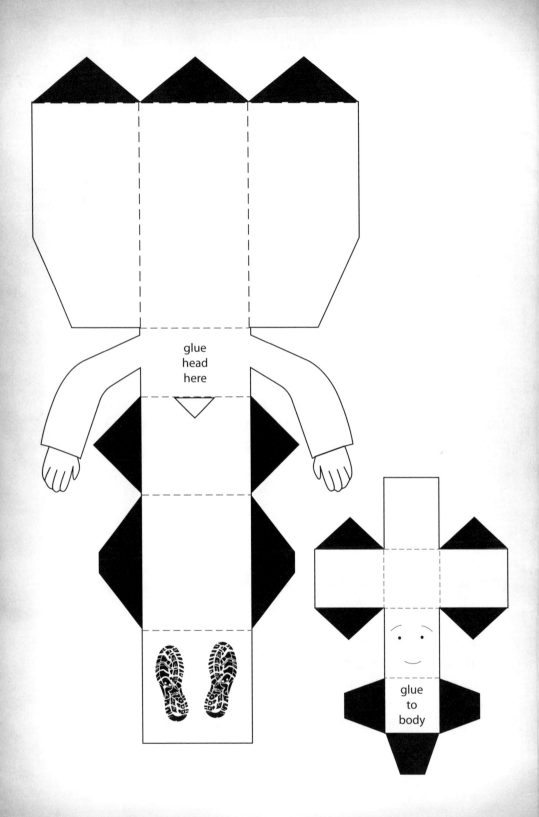

glue
head
here

glue
to
body

You are a blind, homeless person who begs for a living. You desperately want to see. You've been trying to regain your sight for years, visiting free medical clinics when you can. You are poor and don't have many friends.

You are a prostitute who feels like you have no other way of making a living. People look down on you. They cross the road when you walk by so they don't have to pass you on the street. You know you're worth more than they think, and wish someone would give you a fresh start in life. You have very little money and few friends.

You are an NFL star with a great future ahead of you. You've had teams fighting over you, trying to sign you once your current contract expires. You earn tons of money and have a beautiful wife and family.

You are a politician, elected to serve in Congress. Your party is in power, and you get to influence important decisions about how the country is run.

You are a high school math teacher. You enjoy your job, and you're good at it. You love having the opportunity to influence the next generation, and you're good at supporting students who are going through difficult circumstances at home.

You are a well-known supermodel who is in high demand. You spend most of your time flying around the globe to fashion shoots and catwalk shows. Your picture has appeared on the front cover of popular magazines. However, because you're away so much, it's hard to sustain a relationship, and you have just broken up with your second husband

You are a child who lives on the streets in Calcutta, India. You have never been to school. You earn money by begging from cars when they stop at the traffic lights. You live in a shelter with your parents and brothers and sisters.

You are a high school student. You have a learning disability—dyslexia—and so you struggle to keep up with your work. You're often bored at school and disruptive in class, and you get into trouble with teachers. You have just returned to school after a three-day suspension. Your mom and dad are trying to help you sort things out.

You are the pastor of a small country church in a rural community. You are married with three children. You are also the principal of the county's only elementary school. You enjoy playing guitar in your spare time.

You are a dance student who is determined to make dancing your career even though you know you will never make much money from it. You work at McDonald's to help pay your way through college and are grateful for the extra money your mom gives you sometimes. Your parents divorced when you were young, and you haven't heard from your dad in years.

You are a retiree who fought in World War II, serving in the Navy. You live in a nursing home. Your son visits you once or twice a year. You use a wheelchair to get around and don't get out very often.

You are a young single mom who lives on her own with her two-year-old son. You dropped out of school when you got pregnant, but you managed to get your GED by taking night classes at the library. You live on welfare and food stamps at the moment, but you hope to get work as a secretary once your son goes to preschool.

You are a movie star who first became famous in a long-running TV sitcom. Your marriage ended very publicly when your actor husband left you for his co-star in a film. You haven't had a long-term relationship since, and you haven't had any good film roles either. At least you've got millions of dollars to live on!

You won a reality TV music show and produced a number-one single. You then spent the following year working really hard on your first album so you wouldn't be a one-hit wonder. It worked—your album ended up to be the fastest selling CD of all time.

You work in computer technology and really enjoy your job. You've just been promoted to head of your department. You are married with two children, enjoy playing golf, and love inviting friends and neighbors over for backyard cookouts.

You have just finished a degree in medicine. You've decided to put your career on hold at the moment so you can work as a volunteer in a refugee camp in Africa. Working in Africa is hard and dangerous, but you know that you're making a difference to the people you are helping.

You used to be the president of the United States. Now you're devoting your life to bringing about peace in the Middle East. Since leaving the White House, you've had to learn how to use a cell phone and e-mail.

You are a businesswoman who set up a chain of shops selling beauty products. You are determined to do business in a way that is just and fair. You sell fair-trade products when you can and are honest about what your products can do—instead of claiming they can reduce wrinkles. You are single but have a close community of friends and family around you.

You are a high school junior and are enjoying life. You get good grades and are pretty sure you'll get a good scholarship for college. You're in a rock band with some of your friends and would love to be a professional guitarist, but you know it's hard to make a career out of playing guitar. Your parents hope you'll give up the music when you go to college so you can pursue a more serious career choice.

You are a traffic cop, and it's your job to catch people who are parking in the wrong place. Your job is very unpopular, and people often shout rude things at you when they discover you have given them a ticket.

Failure?

Read this aloud together in your small group, taking turns reading:

Peter, One of Jesus' Disciples:

I can't quite believe what has happened over the last few days. It's like my whole world has collapsed around me.

I'm Peter, one of Jesus' disciples. For the last three years, we spent most days together. There was a group of us who went around with him, listening to his teaching, watching the miracles, seeing the way that he treated people. Jesus was always talking about his Father's kingdom and how people could know God. It was really exciting and it all seemed to be building up to something.

A week ago Jesus rode into Jerusalem on a donkey. There were crowds of people by the side of the road, cheering, shouting his name, waving palm branches. It was amazing! Then a few days later, Jesus started talking about his death. He said that he was going to be betrayed. We didn't really know what to make of all of that. I promised Jesus that I would never betray him, and I really meant it. But Jesus said that I would.

Later that week we celebrated the Passover feast all together, and it was obvious that Jesus knew something was about to happen. During the meal he broke the bread and passed around the wine and said that we were to do that in memory of him. I didn't understand…why did we need something to remember him by when he was with us?

After the meal we went out for a walk to an olive grove where we'd been before. And suddenly a bunch of soldiers arrived with Judas. Judas was one of Jesus' disciples, but he ended up turning him in. They took Jesus away to the high priest's house. I followed—after all, I'd promised to stick with Jesus. I waited in the courtyard outside. And that's when I chickened out.

I'm so ashamed of myself. Someone asked me if I was with Jesus, and I said no. Then someone else asked, and I said no again. Then a third person asked. I denied Jesus three times, just like Jesus had said. And there was nothing I could do to help Jesus anyway. The priests wanted him dead. Pilate, the Roman leader, agreed to sentence him to death. And so they crucified him yesterday. I watched from a distance, and I could see how much he was suffering. Then he died.

So here I am now. It's the Sabbath day, our day of rest, so all I can do is sit here and think about what's happened. My mind has just been going around and around in circles all day. We thought that things were going to change. We thought that Jesus was going to be the leader in this new kingdom that he kept talking about. But it's all gone wrong. It's all over.

Talk about these questions together:

- What's your gut reaction to this part of the story?

- Imagine you were Peter. What would you have felt or thought after these events? What would you have felt or thought after you saw Jesus tortured and killed?

- Step into the story right at this point. Would you consider Jesus a success or a failure? Why?

Prayer Cord

You'll need one length of cord (about 2 feet long) and seven beads.

1. Tie a knot about 5 inches from one end of the cord.

2. Thread a bead onto the longer end of the cord from the knot.

3. Tie a second knot on the other side of the bead so that it is caught between two knots. If the hole in the bead is quite large, you may need to double the knot to hold it in place.

4. For your second bead, tie a knot about 1 inch away from your first bead. Thread the second bead on, and secure it with another knot on its other side.

5. Continue attaching the beads to the cord, with a knot on each side, leaving about 1 inch between the beads.

When your cord has seven beads on it, tie the two ends together in a tight knot. Cut the free ends of the cord so they're even.

You're done!

The beads represent the seven areas of life you explored today:

- Shopping and Buying
- Church
- School
- Work
- Areas of Need
- Recreation and Entertainment
- Creative Expression

This is how you pray using your prayer cord:

You hold the cord in one hand. Take a bead between your thumb and index finger and say a prayer for the area of life that it represents. Then move on to the next bead, and so on round the cord. This cord can be used to pray "Your Kingdom come" (see Matthew 6:9-13) in each of the seven categories of life. Ask God to show you how you can be faithful to him in each of those areas of your life.